Chasing the Dream!

How to Grow a Business in these Amazing Times

CHRIS BEKS

Published by Chris Beks 2020
Copyright © 2019 Chris Beks

www.ceebeks.com

All rights reserved. No part of this publication may be reproduced, stored in a retrieval system, or transmitted in any form or by any means, electronic, mechanical, photocopying, recording or otherwise, without the prior written permission from the publisher.

Disclaimer

Every effort has been made to ensure that this book is free from error or omissions. Information provided is of general nature only and should not be considered legal or financial advice. The intent is to offer a variety of information to the reader. However, the author, publisher, editor or their agents or representatives shall not accept responsibility for any loss or inconvenience caused to a person or organisation relying on this information.

A catalogue record for this book is available from the National Library of Australia.

Book cover design and formatting services by BookCoverCafe.com

ISBN 978-0-6484082-0-8

You are right in the middle of a really critical time. You will either fall back or fly forward. And it's all dependent on one thing; what you choose to say yes to right now. Here's where your choices will get tested. Your fears will convince you that new choices will take you so far out of your comfort zone that you won't be able to cope. They'll send your mind into a spin until you succumb to paralysis; numbing you from experiencing excitement of your evolution. Because your fears don't know your strengths. They do not have any clue about the potential that is right before you. They are coming up right now because you know you are ready for more, but you have one foot in your past and another in your future. Your soul is tugging you to move forward whilst your fears are grabbing hold of your ankle, manipulating you into the comfort of staying small. The longer you stand in limbo, the quicker the mind war will buckle your legs from its weight. Save yourself the breakdown. Say yes to the next best steps. You've got this.

— **Colette Werden** – *@ColetteWerden/www.colettewerden*

Dedication

My very first book is dedicated to Sister Marg (from the Sisters of Mercy Order in Shepparton), who taught Year 10-12 Accounting and encouraged me to become an accountant about forty years ago. Way back in 1977 she said to me "you will make a good accountant, Mr Beks, if you decide to pursue a career in accounting, because you get it".

To my life partner, Angela and our daughters, Dinah, Alli & Sofie for their encouragement and support in this project and in life!

To Paul Dunn, for creating my 'epiphany', for his friendship and his continuing mentoring role.

And to the team, customers and friends of Ceebeks Business Solutions for GOOD for teaching me and allowing me to teach them along this journey.

Thank you.

Contents

Dedication	iv
Foreword	ix
Introduction	xi

Part One — 1

Chapter 1 — 3
Having the right business structure before you start

Chapter 2 — 9
The purpose of a business
- Why are You in business? — 10
- Did you have an 'entrepreneurial seizure'? — 12
- So how do you turn this thinking around? — 14

Chapter 3 — 18
How business in these amazing times is different
- Why you do what you do matters more than what you do — 19
- The challenge is to matter more — 20

Chapter 4 — 23
The 4 ways to grow your business
- Let's look at why this can have such a dramatic impact on your business. — 24

Chapter 5 — 27
The First Way – Increase the number of customers (*of the type you want*)
- Why it matters — 30

    Who's your ideal customer?   31
    Making the ideal customer come alive with personas   32

Chapter 6   35
The Second Way – Increase the number of times customers come back

    Developing relationships to build your business   37
    Awesome service removes perceived indifference   37
    Customer complaints are 'gold'   38
    A responsive CRM is crucial for nurturing customers   43
    Team commitment   45
    The value of newsletters, blogs and 'community' groups   50
    Classify your customers in value segments   52
    The Power of Customer Advisory Boards   53

Chapter 7   56
The Third Way – Increase Your Average Sale of Each Sale

    Some easy ways to increase your average sale   59
    Three Levels of pricing   65
    Package together your products or services   66
    Educating your customer to buy   71
    Margins and Prices   72
    Price versus value and service   73

Chapter 8   84
The Fourth Way – Improve the 'Processes' within Your Business

    What happens when you get to the end when you know it's finally complete?   87

Creating 'The Way We Do It Here'	89
Working **ON** not **IN**	90
Develop procedures manuals	91
Performance standards for your phone	92
What about a Collection System?	95
'Until further notice' agreements	96
Complete your SWOT analysis	96
Building an amazing business is all about moments of connection	97
The importance of team	98

Part Two — 101
Seven major areas to help you win new customers

Section 1	103
Advertising & letter writing to help you win new customers	
Section 2	112
UCD's – are they still relevant?	
Section 3	116
Sales systems & techniques	
Consider using the '6 Questions Test'	121
Section 4	129
The phone	
Section 5	132
Other promotions	
Section 6	137
Junk Mail – may not be junk after all!	
What Should You Look For?	140

Section 7 — 142
Become a key person of influence
Final thoughts — 145

Part Three — 149

Appendix 1 — 151
Using 3 Ways to Dramatically Grow Your Business

Appendix 2 — 153
Your Own Ideal Customer Persona Traits Template

Appendix 3 — 155
A Sales System Example
- Scenario 1 — 156
- Scenario 2 — 156

Appendix 4 — 159
The '6 Questions Test'
- 6 Questions You Need to Ask Your Event Entertainment Crew and How Memorable Events Answers Them — 164

Appendix 5 — 168
Positive cash flow and good debtor control

Appendix 6 — 178
Margin Tables

Appendix 7 — 181
Performance Standards for your Phone

Acknowledgements — 188
About the Author — 189
Special Offer — 191

Foreword

These are amazing times.

You and I have never experienced times like them before.

Things move so fast, attention spans decrease, we're 'on' 24 hours a day. First thing in the morning we switch on the phone for what we think might be messages and world news perhaps. But we're actually switching on for the 'hit' of dopamine the phones give us. And amazingly enough, we even take them out (as in out of our pockets) on dates!

But underneath it all, when you STOP, you see some things stay the same even though we don't normally notice they do.

Things like caring, things like perseverance, things like REALLY listening, REALLY connecting.

And that's why this book is so timely and so good — because Chris Beks oozes all of those things.

He shows it every single day in his fantastic 'Chasing the Dream' blog. Thousands and thousands of words written principally for his local community. Literally hundreds upon hundreds of insights. And each post absolutely both first AND world class.

So this book is more than just 'a book'. It's Chris 'coming out' beyond his local community and effectively saying 'Hey world. Stop, listen (well, read) and learn.'

You'll be so glad you did just that.

Because right here you'll find (again) not just 'a book' but a recipe – a recipe for a hugely (not mildly but hugely) successful business.

If there were a Michelin star for recipes in books, this one would surely win several!

When you follow Chris's recipe, when you grab the ingredients, when you mix them and when you bake them together (by actually applying them), the dream you started out chasing when you dreamt of your first business becomes reality. Right here. Right now.

And to extend the recipe analogy just a little, there's that old quote about not having your cake and eating it.

That's completely untrue here.

You get it all, no holds barred, perfectly delivered and absolutely ready for you to get your teeth into. Again, right here. Right now.

Get out your highlight pen (you may need more than one) and come on this journey to a much better business with Chris. I can promise you you'll love where it takes you.

Paul Dunn

Introduction

In 1990, our business solutions enterprise started, we 'hung up our shingle' and wanted to make a real difference on lives – in fact, we wanted to change the world by changing one person's lifestyle at a time.

We wanted to become known as the 'Lifestyle' Accountants who impact lives.

We believe that every business has the ability to impact lives no matter how big those businesses are and love the idea of the power of small contributions that can make an enormous impact.

Like most accountants, we provided a service offering all of the traditional accounting types things – but we weren't satisfied with doing the ordinary things, we wanted to do the extraordinary things...

... and we wanted to matter more.

But this all changed back in 1999, when I attended a boot camp.

This was not a boot camp for fitness nuts or one promoting the latest new diet fad by a health guru, this was a special boot camp for Accountants.

Yes, an Accountants boot camp.

Now before you start conjuring up bizarre images in your mind of bespectacled, grey, balding old men in pinstripe suits running around obstacles clutching their calculators and spread sheets – this was no ordinary boot camp!

Whilst we were pushed out of our comfort zones and challenged in our thinking to break the traditional old mould of how things were always done in our profession, this boot camp was like an epiphany for me.

It was a life-changing event because it not only reinforced my awareness of just how powerful my profession is (as we have the ability to transform and impact people's lives) but this boot camp provided us with new tools and a mindset to do this – rather than just doing tax!

This boot camp was run by master presenter and 4-time TEDx speaker Paul Dunn and his Results Corporation team.

Paul and his team clearly articulated how to grow a business and broke it down into 4 main areas and this thinking really resonated with me and still does today.

New skills were developed by our business as a result of these new insights, new accreditations in financial planning, loan writing, SMSF and Aged Care were obtained because the demand for more than tax services was required.

But being able to show customers the basic fundamentals for how to grow a business always provided the greatest reward and satisfaction for me and our team.

I remain forever grateful for the opportunity to attend the 'boot camp' event as it has enabled me to provide so much more to our customers, improve their business, their lives and their family's lifestyle.

INTRODUCTION

Today, when we meet a new customer, conversation about how they are running their business quickly moves to outlining the use of 4 basic principles as the guiding force for creating quick wins and future successes – which they love to learn about.

By focusing on proven business building strategies and new ideas, I hope this book helps you discover the opportunities right at your doorstep and tackle the challenges holding you back. And in doing so, helps you build an even better business so your business grows, your profits improve, and your life and lifestyle get better!

I am really confident that by focusing on some of the ideas in this book, particularly defining why you do what you do, creating a business that matters and the 4 ways to grow your business, you will change your thinking and the way of looking at your business; and experience growth (both personal and business) that you may not have been able to achieve before, and make your own impact on the world.

After all you are chasing your dream of building a better lifestyle for you and your family, aren't you?

Remember, however, that the power of any idea is only as effective as its implementation. So ensure that you take an idea from this book – any idea – and implement it.

In this way, implementing ideas and tweaking them for maximum results will become habit forming and a natural part of your role as entrepreneur.

I would love to know if this book matters and makes a difference for you – do let me know your results if this book has an impact on your business, your family and your life. You can send me an email here: chris@ceebeks.com

Good luck as you chase your dream!

Part One

Chapter 1

Having the right business structure before you start

Before you start chasing your dream you need to make some time to understand which business structure is right for you.

Regardless of whether I am working with an existing business or a new business, the approach I have is to firstly understand the business and its operating environment. The second area I look at is the financial and personal objectives of the owners and thirdly review their existing legal structures and/or discuss the proposed business structure alternatives.

If it is an existing business, I review the history and structure of ownership and how effective those structures currently are in five important areas:

1. Protecting what you own – your assets
2. Minimising your income tax (and capital gains tax)
3. Simplifying your administration
4. Achieving your retirement goals and
5. Setting out your estate planning objectives

For existing business structures, I identify any entities that have outlived their useful life and, subject to any adverse tax and stamp duty considerations, and then look to wind them up.

I believe people should have efficient business structures and these structures need to be able to justify their existence and effectiveness.

A couple of years ago, I had a family come to see me who owned a big dairy farm. They had a flow chart of all their legal structures, and there were arrows going everywhere to various business structures like companies and trusts etc.

What stuck in my mind was the farmer said to me "Beksy, all we're trying to do is grow some livestock, milk cows and live a comfortable life without paying too much tax along the way".

You can see how a situation like that can arise over the course of many years and several generations. As extra family members are admitted to the business, accountants and solicitors sometimes keep adding structures and it all becomes more complex and, ultimately, unwieldy.

In a very simple world with no adverse income tax or asset protection considerations to worry about, the best and most simple structure would be for everybody to trade as a sole trader, or a partnership if there is more than one owner.

But, unfortunately, we live in a much more complex and litigious world and there are such considerations and that is why accountants and solicitors sometimes advise business owners to have more sophisticated (and more complex) legal trading structures.

CHAPTER 1: HAVING THE RIGHT BUSINESS STRUCTURE BEFORE YOU START

There is no 'one size fits all' solution though, and the right structure will depend on two important considerations:

- asset protection, and
- the ability to 'split' income with family members and reduce the overall tax rate.

The degree to which asset protection is important to you depends on the type of business you are in or going into.

It is always good to ensure you only have the structures you need. This is so true now more than ever before because the administration requirements or 'red tape' in business have increased, not decreased – and so has the cost to maintain them.

For example, it will be more important to protect your other assets (business and personal) the higher the possibility your trading business could incur liabilities for:

- events not covered by business insurances
- financial failure, or
- occupational health and safety issues.

In such a situation trading as a sole trader or partnership of individuals would not be considered a suitable business structure, as your assets would be exposed to unsecured business creditors.

The general principle is that trading activities are best carried out by trusts, companies or a partnership of trusts and their assets should be confined to core trading assets only – all other assets should be kept separate and held by other legal structures.

As you can see from the example above, if maximising asset protection and minimising income tax are key considerations for you, your business structures may need to be more complex than you would otherwise like them to be.

Here are four factors for choosing business structures:

1. The right structure for you will depend on your personal situation and circumstances – this is stating the obvious, but there really is no 'one size fits all' solution.
2. Separate your business trading assets from your business wealth assets. This can be a suitable risk management strategy in some circumstances and means you may trade in one entity and hold your wealth assets (e.g. business real estate, trademarks etc) in another entity. If the business encounters financial difficulty, these business wealth assets and your personal assets (other than those secured by lenders) are better protected if they are owned by a separate legal structure.
3. Retain sufficient profits in the business to finance future activities, but transfer any remaining profits out. Transfer remaining profits of the trading business to an external investment structure or structures, for example an investment discretionary trust or company. Again this is a risk management strategy and will vary depending on the business because some businesses have to retain

more profits than others to fund their expansion, particularly businesses in capital-intensive industries. Have a policy on to what extent you will gear so you can use a mix of your own funds and borrowed funds to fund expansion. Borrowing some funds allows you to get the rest of your wealth out and into other safe, tax-effective and wealth-creating structures.

Many people do this through superannuation, but not all, particularly young people who quite rightly don't want to have funds locked away for 20 or 30 years when they have houses to build and children to educate. They may have an alternative structure such as a discretionary trust. As always, the right business structure will depend on your personal circumstances.

4. Regard your employment in the business as separate to your ownership of the business. Think of yourself wearing the 'hats' of two people – owner and employee.

This is important for a number of reasons, including:

- to maintain financial equitable arrangements between owners working in the business and those who do not
- to ensure any conflicts of interest in decision making between 'employee owners' and 'non-employee owners' are transparent and managed having regard to the best interests of the business
- to accurately calculate the value of the business.

> **Chasers Tip**   Get some advice, spend some money & get the right structure at the start!

Before the chase begins, it really is worth investing a little time and money to get this right.

At the start of chasing your dream it will save you time, money and give you peace of mind knowing you have protected your investment in the long run.

Chapter 2

The purpose of a business

Consultant Alan Weiss describes the purpose of a business is to offer value (through products and/or services) to customers, who pay for the value with cash or equivalents. At a minimum, the money received should cover the costs of operating the business as well as provide for the life needs of the owner.

Peter Drucker famously wrote in *The Practice of Management* that the purpose of a business is to create and keep a customer.

While his main point about the purpose of a business may indeed be true, it's the bare minimum and something that's required to keep the doors open. I think to aim there as the purpose of a business is to shoot terribly low.

I believe the purpose of a business is to matter and create meaning, which allows a niche of followers who 'get' your meaning to buy from you and, in doing so, reward you and allow you then to make a contribution to better the lives of those less fortunate around the world.

In other words to make a difference to ourselves, our customers and to our global family!

Bernadette Jiwa in her book *'Meaningful'* puts it beautifully this way "Our job is not simply to obsess about the features and benefits of what we're making: it is to wonder and care about the difference we can make to people and to our world".

So, what does this mean for your business?

Can you discover a purpose greater than simply creating a customer; can you create a business, a culture, built to communicate that purpose?

What might change if you did?

What has to change if you do?

What organisations could you model your working 'on purpose' business upon?

How can you draw people to commit and connect to your reason for existing?

Why are You in business?

'The two most important days in your life are the day you are born and the day you find out why' – Mark Twain

What got you started?

What was the motivational factor that pushed you into the realm of self-employment?

How did you get your entrepreneurial juices flowing?

What was your business-owning epiphany?

CHAPTER 2: THE PURPOSE OF A BUSINESS

To borrow a favourite 'Star Wars' theme, the 'force' must have been strong in you to make you give up the comfort, security and regularity of that weekly pay cheque and the 9 to 5 routine!

Why did you want to go into business?

Statistics show the small businesses that start up from scratch don't have a very good survival rate. If you knew that you only had a 60% chance of surviving the first 12 months would you do it?

Sound a bit negative?

Well, it's important to know that if you do get past that first year you will have an 80% chance of failing in the first 7 years. To top that off statistics show that in the next 7 years you have an 80% chance of becoming being non-existent.

So the statistical evidence is against you right from the very start!

Why don't a lot of small businesses work?

If you can answer this question then you have the magic key needed to make sure your business does not become a statistic. Yes, it is true that small businesses are failing at an alarmingly high rate, but yours doesn't have to be one of them.

Each year, millions of small businesses are started and many of them have little chance of succeeding. But what is this phenomenon where do they come from?

Well, many of them have been "working for someone else."

These people could be highly paid lawyers, doctors to architects, hairdressers or plumbers and electricians. The common theme in nearly all cases is that they are sick of what they do, but the technical work of their profession is what they do best.

Did you have an 'entrepreneurial seizure'?

In the words of Michael Gerber in his best-selling book *The E-Myth Revisited—Why Most Small Businesses Don't Work and What to Do About It*—most people, just like you and me, suffered an 'entrepreneurial seizure'!

'My boss is an idiot', 'If it weren't for me this place wouldn't exist', 'Anybody can run a business and I'll guarantee you I can do it better than the people upstairs'.

And so they quit their job to start a business that will give them a lifestyle, freedom and the money to do what they want to do.

The assumption that they understand the business because they understand – and maybe are experts at – the technical work of the business. They think because they know the work, they are qualified to run the business.

But this could not be further from the truth!

Then reality sets in and they're 'doing it, doing it, doing it all and instead of creating utopia for themselves they have created a business 'hell'!

By starting their own business they move from a job they are very capable, maybe even fantastic at, to the same role plus 20 others which they know almost nothing about.

After the convulsions of the seizure have finished and the smoke has cleared what is left? A would-be entrepreneur with the skills of a technician now a part of the business world – and in trouble, big, big trouble!

Have you seen, first hand, examples of this?

CHAPTER 2: THE PURPOSE OF A BUSINESS

I'm willing to bet you either have or know someone who has because it really is so common.

You know, your girlfriend (the hairdresser) who quit her job last year to start her own salon or your mate (the plumber) who told his boss to 'stick it' about 6 months ago and started his own plumbing business. No longer do you get to see them as frequently as you would like to because they are flat out trying to keep up with all of the aspects of running a business – managing cash flow, chasing up overdue debtors, answering the phone, making appointments, instructing and leading team members, scheduling work, doing the work, sending out invoices, preparing marketing campaigns etc.

In the words of Michael Gerber – they're 'doing it, doing it, doing it'!

... or is this You?

This is what working *in* your business means.

You're in the midst of it and trying to handle everything and be everything to everybody.

Now close your eyes and picture this instead...

You've taken a few steps back from your business and you're looking at it objectively, saying, 'Without me, what would happen? What do I want to happen? What needs to be done to free me up from working *IN* it all the time?'

If your business were a movie, who would be the supporting actors, what would the ending look like?

Just thinking about it, you can sense the huge difference this could make.

Imagine taking some time away from day-to-day tasks and looking at your business in the long term.

Think of the creative ideas or opportunities you could come up with!

This is working ON your business.

The secret is not to work IN your business, but to work ON it.

So how do you turn this thinking around?

Well, a great place to start is to simply change your thinking about your role in the business – as opposed to you being the business. Your business provides the product or service that you sell and your role is to manage and make this happen in the most efficient manner possible.

The key to creating a great business starts with knowing that it is your business that is the true product and not what produce or service you deliver.

The most important aspect of your business is you. You are not your business and your business is not you.

To understand the bigger picture that will fuel your business growth you must answer a number of questions about you personally:

- What do you want your life to look like?
- What type of person do you want to become?
- What is most important to you in your life?
- At the end of your life, what would you like people to remember you for?

CHAPTER 2: THE PURPOSE OF A BUSINESS

- What skills would you like to acquire before your life is over?
- How would you like to look and feel physically?
- How much money will you need to earn to live the life you want?
- When will you need this money?

The primary aim is the vision for your life that your business can help you fulfil. It is a purpose that keeps you focused and gives you the energy to do what you have to do, especially through the tough times you are bound to experience.

Steven R Covey describes this visualisation of your business as 'starting with the end in mind' in his book, *The 7 Habits of Highly Successful People*.

In other words, whenever you start a process, understand exactly what the end point is before you start.

Think about that in the context of a business. How many business owners actually do that?

Why did you go into business?

Financial independence?

To be your own boss?

To spend more time with your family?

Is it happening for you?

The fact is, most of us jump or fall into business. Before we know it, we are so busy we have no time to think about what we want from the business, how it will be shaped and what it will be like the day we retire or sell it.

End-in-mind thinking makes a profound difference. You should spend some time visualising what your completed, finished, ready-to-sell-if-you-wanted-to business looks or will look like in order to fully grasp this idea.

If your business were complete, done and ready to sell (even if you don't want to) – what would it look like?

Once you start to think about your business like this and establish clearly in your mind the end game, you can then work backwards to put in place the strategies, systems, processes and people required to get you there.

When we think about how to grow our businesses by standing out, staying competitive and relevant, we often begin by wondering how to use the latest technology to do this. While we can't foresee a future that hasn't yet arrived, we *can* act on the things we know that remain the same and are constant. Our customers that we serve will always want to be appreciated and acknowledged, valued and loved. If we begin with that end in mind too then we will be on the right path.

An American author, entrepreneur, marketer, and public speaker whom I have great respect for is Seth Godin. I love his take on growing a business using just two words – First ten, which he describes simply as the secret of the new marketing. *'Find ten people. Ten people who trust you/respect you/need you/listen to you...'*

Those ten people need your services, what you have to sell, or just simply want it. And if they love it, you win – it's that simple really! And if they really, really love it, they'll each find you ten more people if you just ask them to (or a hundred or a thousand or, perhaps, just three).

To grow then you just need to repeat this over and over again!

What if they don't love your services or products or want it?

Well in that case you need new services or products.

So you will need to reinvent, re-innovate or simply start all over again.

CHAPTER 2: THE PURPOSE OF A BUSINESS

Your idea spreads. Your business grows. Not as fast as you want, but faster than you could ever imagine.

This approach changes the posture and timing of everything you do.

You no longer market to the anonymous masses because they're not unknown anymore and they're not masses. You can only market to people who are willing participants – like this group of ten (and those that they refer to you).

The timing means that the idea of a 'launch' and press releases and the big unveiling is just crazy and no longer relevant.

Instead, plan on generating hype around your services or products, a groundswell, the gradual build that turns into a tidal wave.

Organise for it and spend money accordingly.

This marketing approach works today really well.

Three years from now though, this advice will be so commonplace and boring because everyone will be doing it. But today, it's almost certainly the opposite of what you're doing, and more importantly, what your competition is doing!

Having advocates and developing them into 'raving lunatics' about your brand, services and products is therefore the key here!

So let's look at some basic principles that you must understand before you can build this business that you can now clearly see!

Chasers Tip Get hold of a copy of the books mentioned in this chapter and read them for a better understanding of your purpose.

Chapter 3

How business in these amazing times is different

About two years ago, we saw millennials officially overtake baby boomers as the largest living generation, and are expected to comprise seventy-five per cent of the workforce by 2025.

Given their sheer mass, combined with their shifting professional goals, this generation is changing the way we have traditionally done and think about business.

Our three teenage daughters are part of this group and we are seeing it first-hand how different they view the world and their role in it! Even though they only have part-time jobs after school, our three girls want to make more of a contribution to society than their work and are not prepared to settle for these roles as a future career – they too want to make a difference.

No longer is it acceptable to do business 'the way it's always been done' – in the eyes of this generation they will challenge this old way of thinking and look to turn things on their head to find a better, smarter, efficient and quicker way of getting things done! They constantly ask why it is done that way once they understand what has to be done and then look for a smarter, more efficient and often more cost effective way to do it.

This generation will radically disrupt traditional businesses and threaten those that refuse to change and adapt! They will take up a greater share of the market if competitors remain ignorant of their style and thinking.

Thanks to millennials, a business's 'cause' has become as important, if not more so, than its profit-making potential. In an article in *The Huffington Post*, almost all millennials surveyed – ninety-four per cent – have said that they want to use their skills to benefit a cause. And more than half have said they'd actually take a pay cut to find work that matches their values.

Why you do what you do matters more than what you do

So, especially in the coming years, a business's 'cause' will become a powerful factor for attracting talent.

That's why redefining with a laser focus your purpose, creating a business that matters, your 'WHY' for existing or for starting your business in the first place will likely pay off for you as never before, by bringing you loyal, cause-conscious customers.

Ninety-one percent of millennials – who are an exceptionally brand-loyal generation – have said on surveys that they would switch brands to patronise a competitor that better aligns with their beliefs.

Now this is a HUGE opportunity for businesses that get this!

Better still you can create a niche that relates specifically to millennials if your 'WHY' is aligned with these cause-supporting consumers.

Especially with millennials demanding change in the world and calling the shots then, a business that cares about the world, a business with a purpose is going to be what sets your business apart.

It will bring talent to the door, polishes your brand's image and attracts new customers and keeps them coming back. But becoming a purpose-first business won't happen overnight – it takes patience and practice.

The challenge is to matter more

Instead of trying to make your business appeal to everyone, try to narrow your focus on a niche, be irresistible to a specific group of people. Instead of marketing to the masses

'Why' you do what you do is a concept that will be explored a bit further in the next chapter but for now it's related to your higher purpose, the reason you started your business in the first place – why you exist.

Here are three ways to put your business's purpose front and centre:

1. Bring your 'WHY' to team meetings.
   Shift every conversation away from transactional language at regular team meetings to how you're helping others and tapping

CHAPTER 3: HOW BUSINESS IN THESE AMAZING TIMES IS DIFFERENT

into the purpose, your WHY, your reason for existing. To kick off the meeting, ask everyone in the room to share a "why moment" they experienced in the recently or in past week.

2. When purpose or 'WHY' and talent come together, everybody wins. Make social responsibility the new bottom line.

   It's not always easy to credibly live your purpose, but some business priorities must top quarterly profits.

   I remember reading about a great example of this by outdoor company, Patagonia. At its own expense, they studied the number of synthetic microfibers released into the waterways as its jackets are washed. It found the annual impact to water organisms to be the equivalent of 11,900 plastic bags.

   The company is now on a mission to address the problem, helping to clean up both the planet and its environmentally conscious image.

3. Help your team make it personal

   Make team members a part of what you believe in by telling them your business's story every chance you get. Then, offer them the chance to carry it forward. By involving them in important social responsibility issues they start to focus more clearly on the tasks required as the goal is a common cause for all of us.

   Our lifetime membership in global giving initiative, B1G1 – Business for Good, gives our team the opportunity to personify the reason we get up every morning. Team members are also encouraged to help our community however they see fit, whether through

Greenpeace beach clean ups, helping out with Rotary's Adopt-a-highway clean up or 'Food Share' volunteering or other methods.

All entrepreneurs and small business owners, like you and me, start their business on a mission to make the world a better place, but the struggles of business make those dreams easy to forget.

If you personalise the mission you are on, live it in your business every day and incorporate it within the community in which you live, others will want to be a part of it and join in.

We have seen this work first hand and now have a group of customers who regularly put their hand up to help us with these community based initiatives whenever we put the call out for help!

For example, just last Easter our team organised an Easter Hamper drive to supplement the weekly food hampers prepared by Food Share volunteers to include some Easter goodies like chocolate Easter eggs, chocolate Easter bunnies and yummy hot cross buns. We were inundated with so many generous donations of chocolate and had a local Bakers Delight franchise provide fresh hot cross buns to those less fortunate in our local community.

It is safe to say that the recipients of the food hampers' Easter will be that little bit more special this year.

> **Chasers Tip** Check out B1G1 – Business for good website at www.b1g1.com to see how you can create a purpose for your business like others here have.

Chapter 4

The 4 ways to grow your business

When it comes down to a simple formula to run a successful business, there are really only four fundamental ways to grow your business: win new customers, get them to come back to you more often, get them to spend more when they do, and improve the processes in your business to ensure that you achieve the first 3.

So that's:

1. Increase the number of customers (*of the type you want*);
2. Increase the number of times they deal with you;
3. Increase your average sale or 'transaction value.'
4. Improve the effectiveness and processes within your business to ensure achievement of the first 3!

When you think about any other strategy, such as cutting costs, it won't *grow* your business unless you use the money you save to promote your business. It may let you control your business better and return greater profits, but it won't *grow* your business.

And what do most businesses focus on?

That's right no.1, winning new customers. And they often ignore the other (usually less expensive) ways to grow their businesses.

If you are a business owner who is almost solely focused on winning new customers, you're missing sales and PROFIT opportunities beyond your wildest dreams!

Let's look at why this can have such a dramatic impact on your business.

Assume you have a customer base of 1,000 who buy from you once a year with an annual spend of $100.

And let's say you can increase the number of inquiries and therefore the number of new customers by 10%. That would mean your customer base would increase to 1,100.

Now, imagine if you increased the number of times your customers dealt with you during their lifetime by again 10%. Let's say from once to 1.1.

Next, you go ahead and, through certain techniques, you manage to increase your average sale or 'transaction value' by 10% as well, this time taking it from $100 to $110.

Now if you were to put all of these factors together, what do you think might happen to your turnover?

CHAPTER 4: THE 4 WAYS TO GROW YOUR BUSINESS

Assuming everything else was equal, it would make sense to say that the overall business would grow by 10%.

Right?

Wrong!

In fact, something completely different happens.

Something that could mean the difference between a profit or a loss for your business or between a comfortable lifestyle and a wealthy one.

For a moment, look at the next calculation. It shows the numbers before any increase and multiplies them to estimate turnover roughly.

Number of customers x Number of dealings x Average $ Sale = Turnover

1,000 x 1 x $100 = $100,000

Look at what happens to turnover when just one area – winning new customers, for example – is increased by 10%.

1,100 x 1 x $100 = $110,000

The same happens when either the number of times your customers deal with you or the average transaction value is increased by 10%.

1,000 x 1.1 x $100 = $110,000

Or…

1,000 x 1 x $110 = $110,000

But look what happens when all three areas are increased by 10% at the same time. That's right – increasing each area at the same time has a multiplier effect of increasing turnover NOT by 10% like you could assume, but by a staggering 33.1%!

An additional income of not 10% to $110,000 but 33.1% to $133,100!

An increase of $33,100 in turnover for doing nothing else except improving EACH area at once rather than concentrating on just one area at a time.

This multiplier effect is caused by the combination, the momentum, of all 3 areas working together. Each impacts the other, if you will.

So once more, rather than a 10% growth factor, the momentum created by working on EACH one of these first key areas brings about a growth of 33.1%!

> **Chasers Tip** In Appendix 1 at the back of this book, there is a worksheet for you to enter your own business numbers. This way you can see at first-hand the impact that applying 3 of the ways to grow your business can have on your own business!

The next four chapters will look in more detail at the four ways of growing your business based on these areas above.

Chapter 5

The First Way – Increase the number of customers (*of the type you want*)

Winning customers is where most business owners focus their marketing energy and it is where it all starts. Given that, then, it's fitting to explore this area first. (Each of the others will be explored in turn in later chapters.)

Before, we delve into this first way of growing a business we need to qualify it with the addition *'of the type you want'*. The reason being is that you don't want to appeal to everyone and anyone because you will just create more problems for yourself. For example, ever dealt with selfish, rude and obnoxious customers or those that whinge and complain and never pay their bills on time or take up most of your time but don't want to pay your price?

Well, that is why we need to qualify the first way to grow a business – Increase the number of customers 'of the type you want' – those that are a real pleasure to help, pay always on time, are positive in nature, are raving fans of what you do and refer your business to their family and friends and are willing to accept your help and advice!

So let's explore how to win more of your ideal type of customer by setting 'the scene' for working out how you go about doing this.

What's an ideal customer?

According Seth Godin, here's what defines an ideal customer:

- A customer who wants your products
- A customer who has the ability to pay for the product
- A customer who has the authority to purchase your product

> **Chasers Tip** Replace 'products' with services if you provide these instead.

An ideal customer of your product/service is a customer who:

- Has a problem you can solve
  If your customer doesn't have the problem you're solving, then she probably arrived there by mistake and will soon leave. Or possibly you're not being very clear on the problem you're solving and you and your customer have a different idea of what it is. In any case, solving a pressing problem your customer has is a requirement at the start for your product/service.

CHAPTER 5: THE FIRST WAY – INCREASE THE NUMBER OF CUSTOMERS (OF THE TYPE YOU WANT)

- Has the same worldview as you
  When they see your product, an ideal customer must experience the 'WOW – oh yeah, moment'. The 'this is for me' feeling. So not only must your product/service solve a problem they are deeply concerned about, but also you need to talk in terms your customer understand – their language. If your product/service messaging is crisp & professional, then your ideal customers will be crisp & professional. If on the other hand, your messaging is laid-back and fun-oriented, so will your ideal customers be.
- Has time & money to use your product/service
  An ideal customer won't complain endlessly that you're too expensive. They'll recognise they're getting enough value from your product to be worth the money you ask for in exchange.
- Is engaged with your product/service
  A customer who never uses your product is bound to leave you because they don't get enough from your product. An ideal customer is engaged with your product, returns to it regularly because they understood the more they used it, the more value they would get, the more successful they become.
- Gets business outcomes from using your product/service
  Most importantly, a customer uses your product to get an outcome – be it personal or business, they are not using it just because. So an important criterion that makes an ideal customer is how your product delivers on this personal or business outcome. Does your product/service make your customer more successful? How can you make your customer even more successful?

Why it matters

If you don't know your ideal customer, it means you only have a vague idea of who you should be marketing to...

... so your marketing becomes vague and diluted. You try to be "all things to all people" and end up convincing nobody. Your product is unfocused and kind of tries to solve a general problem, which makes everyone go to sleep.

You need to take a stand. It means your 'solution' is going to be perfect for one kind of customer. The flip side of the coin is it will repel another kind of customer. But that's okay.

Being bland is a recipe for failure.

Once you know who your ideal customer is, you'll have a clearer direction for your product/service, so that it:

- solves the problem that keeps them up at night
- uses a language they can understand
- is available at a price point they can bear

An ideal customer definition goes hand in hand with a good value proposition. In an ideal customer definition, you know exactly which problem you're solving and why it matters to this customer.

So chances are today your value proposition is not clear and powerful enough, and your ideal customer is not identified.

Who's your ideal customer?

If you already have a customer base, you can extract customers who, for you, are an ideal customer.

You can discover who they are based on engagement or revenue.

And which customers are most engaged with your application or pay you more than others.

If you know which customers are happier with your product/service, you can then determine that they are your ideal customers.

Once you have identified a few customers who you consider to be ideal, try to understand what similarities they share. What makes them ideal customers for your product/service? You want to group them into a segment so that you're confident that a new customer sharing the same attributes will also be ideal (so it means these attributes are what makes an ideal customer for you).

If you don't have a customer base, imagine who your ideal customer could be, based on what you know of the market, people from the market you talked with (customer development interviews). Why would these people be your ideal customers? There is a big guess at work here, so prepare to be wrong and be open to learning (from your customers).

Here are a few questions that can help you think about your different customers:

- How painful is the problem you solve in their life?
- How much money do they have to solve this problem and are they willing to spend it for your product? Do they pay promptly?

- How did they come to you?
- What do they like about doing business with you?
- How do they view their problems?
- What's their definition of value, regarding the problem you're solving?

Making the ideal customer come alive with personas

So maybe you have an idea of who your ideal customer is, but it's still a vague idea. It can help to represent him in a more vivid and concrete way.

That's what a customer persona is for.

Personas are profiles that represent your visitors or customers. You can also call them "customer guess". They are not the profile of any individual customer, but are specific attributes that are representative of a given customer type.

Since we are much better at dealing with the concrete than the abstract, it helps to see your ideal customer as a (fictitious) person.

For example, you would specify:

- their name, occupation, company name
- demographic information
- her values and goals
- the problems she has that your product solves
- the experience she wants when seeking out your product
- her main info sources and watering holes

CHAPTER 5: THE FIRST WAY – INCREASE THE NUMBER OF CUSTOMERS (OF THE TYPE YOU WANT)

- her most common objections to your product
- one day in the life

Do you now have a good idea of who your ideal customer is?

This can be a constant repetitive process but you might find out you don't know enough about your current customers. Doing regular calls and user interviews are a good way to become more customer-centric and learn more about what kind of customers you want.

> **Chasers Tip** In Appendix 2 at the back of this book, there is a template for you to enter your own ideal customer persona traits. This is a critical step in understanding how to apply the 1st of the ways to grow your business!

Having developed a clear strategy for identifying your ideal customer then, how do we go about attracting them?

There are, without a doubt, hundreds upon hundreds of ways to win new customers. So the part Two of this book is devoted to helping you with ideas to do just that. In Sections 1–7 you'll find a list of just some of those key strategies to do just that.

'Client acquisition' – that is, winning new customers – has been the focus of advertising and marketing for many years. To make it easier for you, this list of ideas is broken down further into seven major areas to help you win new customers and to itemise the topics as you begin working through this book.

Chapter 6

The Second Way – Increase the number of times customers come back

This way is designed to give you insight into the massive opportunity that creating a 'back end,' or getting your customers to come back to you over and over, offers your business.

It really represents a huge profit point for your business!

Most business owners focus their marketing energy on winning customers. But getting your customers to come back to your business more often is more vital to the long-term health and profitability of your business. As is increasing your average sale. And that's what you'll learn more about here.

The more frequently your customers purchase from you, the greater your profits. And the greater your profits, the greater the longevity of your business.

Because you paid to acquire that customer on the first sale, every sale after that has no cost to it other than the cost of the goods itself or the labor to complete the service, both of which are covered in the price. So for every sale you make to a past customer, you keep more profits.

It's like the icing on the cake. And it's a huge opportunity for your business.

You see, studies show that it costs six times more to win a new customer than it does to have an existing customer come back and purchase again. As such, if you can build repeat sales for your business, you will be even more profitable again.

Once again, there are many, many ways to encourage your customers to come back. Here you'll find a list of just some of those key strategies to do just that.

'Customer acquisition,' that is, winning new customers, is known as the 'front end.' It's the front of your business, the first time your customers meet you. The front end, or winning new customers, has been the focus of advertising and marketing for many years. Creating a 'back end' – a reason for customers to come back to you over and over, and making sure they do – is just as critical.

This is also known as 'customer retention,' that is, retaining customers and increasing the number of times they deal with you in their 'lifetime.'

Their lifetime is the length of time they deal with you. For example, your average customers might come back to you two or three times over a two-year period.

Developing relationships to build your business

To make it easier for you, we've briefly outlined some ideas to help you get your customers to come back to your business more often.

The first and foremost idea in this area is to simply ask your customers to come back to you.

Most businesses don't bother. They fail to recognise the profit potential this offers a business.

So ask them!

Invite them to come back to your business. Once happy with a product or service or a supplier, most customers want to build on that and keep returning to that business. It's easier for this to happen if customers are given some incentive to do so.

Awesome service removes perceived indifference

Another great way to keep customers coming back to you more often is to offer awesome service. Offer service that goes over and beyond the industry average for your business. Of course, other issues that keep customers coming back are things like having a competitive advantage or better performance than competitors.

So do what you do extremely well, offer better or faster services, provide longer warranties or stronger guarantees, give customers some points to differentiate you from your competitors.

This will make them want to come back.

You see, 68% of customers leave you for another competitor because of something called 'perceived indifference' – customers felt you were indifferent toward them.

You really weren't too concerned whether they bought from you.

Not asking your customers to come back to you, making them offers, and inviting them to do so – all can be perceived as indifference.

So it's important to nurture your relationship with your customers in the same way you would any other relationship that was truly important. Nurturing has got to be one of the most cost-efficient and easiest way to win business from your existing customers. By nurturing your existing customers so that they continue to buy from your business, you are, in fact, saving time and your hard-earned money.

Customer complaints are 'gold'

The aim for one hundred per cent customer satisfaction is like the quest for most forms of perfection – too unrealistic. Problems often happen because the environment in which your business operates changes with the changing wants and needs of customers, market regulation government legislation, global events and so on.

Any business should put processes in place to identify customer satisfaction, put problems right, deliver quality services and products and build better business relationships. The best will invest in effective complaint handling processes recognizing the return in

CHAPTER 6: THE SECOND WAY – INCREASE THE NUMBER OF TIMES CUSTOMERS COME BACK

terms of fully understanding the needs of customers, increased customer loyalty and retention, positive word of mouth advertising and free notification of potential service problems, product failures or non-compliance with regulations and legislation.

Most businesses encourage contact from both customers and team members in one form or another. The monitoring of contacts is vital for effective performance management and, ultimately, better products and services. You will receive suggestions, compliments, product and service enquiries and complaints.

The Australian National Complaints Culture Survey 2000 gathered the opinions of consumers and a variety of businesses. The survey found that 44% of people will now complain all or most of the time when they encounter a problem with a service or purchased goods. Incidence of complaining in a business to business environment is greater than consumer complaints.

An average of only 25-30% of business customers will not pursue a complaint compared to 56% of consumers not making the effort. Interestingly, consumers have a greater tendency to escalate a complaint to a manager or head office. Only 45% of consumers said they complain to the front-line – but 75% of business to business customers complain to a front-line member of staff. Often, a complaint to the front-line goes unrecorded – important information about a product or service is lost.

The number of complaints can also be affected by the perceived loss. A high loss can result in 75% of customers complaining and a low-loss can reduce the figure to 5% or less.

Customers sometimes want written confirmation of action taken but 73% of people would like some personal contact by phone or face to face to quickly resolve the problem – I like this personally too!

You should note that this same survey found 58% of employees expressed dissatisfaction with the level of empowerment given to them to resolve a complaint.

Employees expressed concern about being untrained in complaint handling and being left unsupported. Many said their organisation actively discouraged them from resolving complaints. An unresolved complaint in a business to business environment could be particularly damaging to your business...

Your customers who complain are likely to be regular users of your services or products and their feedback is 'gold' for you because it represents an opportunity, a huge opportunity to prevent future loss of both customers and profits!

A well-handled complaint can actually increase customer loyalty:

- Customers are more likely to use your services again or purchase further products in future (and also sing your praises)
- The use of 1800 numbers for reporting complaints increases customer reporting of problems but also shows your customers that you are sincere in wanting to know about problems (improving your image)
- A study carried out by the Warwick Business School revealed that 53% of examples of outstanding service resulted from complaints handled well by a business.

A well-handled complaint will also:

- educate a customer in the workings of your business
- ensure that your customer will be easier to deal with in future contacts
- be an opportunity for you to impress your customer with your sense of responsibility in business.

Remember the impact a poorly handled complaint can have on business. A customer experiencing difficulties in achieving a resolution is likely to spread bad press about your business:

- Nowadays a dissatisfied customer tells 10 to 25 others about a bad experience
- Internet customers are becoming increasingly aware of the possibilities for tarnishing your image following a poorly-handled complaint (making use of e-mail chat with colleagues and other business partners and even go so far as broadcasting it all over social media!)

A poorly handled complaint can create customers who are badly informed about your business, can be time-consuming for you to handle adequately and force them to go elsewhere.

Ease of complaint reporting can be equally important in making sure that your customers complain in the most cost-effective way. If you have a complaint process that is difficult to access you will find that the process:

- is only accessible to your most knowledgeable customers
- creates difficult customers who may:
- withhold or delay payment
- give up and go elsewhere
- make successive (costly) contacts across your business
- misses out on vital information for your business

The cost of winning new business compared to retaining existing business in these amazing times can be as high as 20 to 1. An effective complaint process will be far-reaching across your business – touching the parts that most other customer retention systems fail to get to!

Your processes will be more customer-focused with customers aiding the business through quick reporting of possible problem areas. You will have a valuable source of information for flagging possible problem areas – ideal for feeding in to quality assurance processes and testing compliance with any relevant regulations and legislation.

When developing or reviewing a complaint process make sure you get the basics right. Easy access to the process is all important. You will need to consider:

- A free-phone help-line for reporting complaints
- Publicity – why not give information on how to complain on invoices or as an insert with contract documents
- Don't limit customers in the ways they communicate problems – perhaps give chat facilities on your website and email contacts

and consider the differing needs of customers in your particular market place – or do you need to have a specific form on your web site for business to business customers to report problems?

Communicate in clear terms – remember a complaint is 'gold' it is a huge opportunity to educate a customer about your products and services. A complaint may highlight that a business partner is not using the full capabilities of a particular product – maybe the customer needs to purchase an additional add-on.

A complaint is an opportunity for you to sell the benefits your business can provide.

Poor communication will cause you to lose out.

A responsive CRM is crucial for nurturing customers

Instead of spending mega dollars on cold canvassing your potential customers, use your 'hot list,' a list of your existing customers, for direct mail, email newsletters and promotions etc.

To start with, it's vital that you collect information about your customers. Phone numbers, email and addresses so that you can stay in touch. In some cases, it's appropriate to gather information about other issues, like theirs, their spouse/partner and kids date of birth, buying patterns, occupation or income levels, favourite sports team and so on.

It's then important to place all of this information in a customer relations management database which allows you to personalise, send, track and monitor. At the very least, hard copy records should be kept, although this is usually more difficult to administer than a digital version. This database could, in fact, be your most valuable asset. For example, if maintained well, a good database can add to the value of the purchase of a business.

Once you've built your database, take the time to stay in touch by sending regular newsletters, offers, vouchers, calendars, service reminder notices, thank you notes, special articles of interest to your customers, Christmas cards, birthday cards, and much more. Each time, build on the relationship you started at the first purchase. *My partner loves scrapbooking in her spare time and she will spend hours personalising hand-made birthday/special occasion cards for our customers – they are always blown away by the intricate care and attention each one is shown!*

Remember, too, that when you do write to your existing customers, it's important to write to them in terms of benefits. And be sure to answer the 'What's In It – For Me?' question in the customers' minds. That way, they find some benefit in coming back to your business. Also, write to them on a personalised, one-on-one basis – greeting them with their name at the beginning of a letter, for example.

Complete follow-up phone calls to make sure they're 100% happy, delighted even, with what they received from your business.

Develop 'communication schedules.' These schedules outline the dates and times of all communications, verbal and written, that you'll send your customers over 1 year, for example. Once again, a good CRM system will save you hours and can be setup to automatically schedule emails, blogs and newsletters to go out whenever you want them to!

We use and love Hubspot for this purpose.

Interestingly, the more often you stay in touch with them, the more often they'll purchase from you. Hence, scheduling communication to reach your customers will bring more of them back into the business.

Offer ongoing education, advice, or support so that customers do have something to come back to and feel that you add value. A well-positioned Facebook Page for your business will allow you to post blogs containing this type of information. This should be aimed at educating your customers, helping customers do, be, or have more because of their purchase.

And it should build on the initial relationship you established and increase repeat sales.

Team commitment

Is your Team on the 'same page'?
Do they know your business's 'WHY'?
Can they simply and clearly articulate why you do what you do?

Creating a 'Team Commitment' can also impress your customers enough to keep them coming back again and again.

A team commitment outlines your team's very real commitment to the customers. It makes certain promises of minimum 'performance standards' and could explain your business ethics and what you commit to do for the customers.

For example, on-time delivery, answer questions and queries at any time, backup services, and more. This tool further differentiates you from your competitors.

It is critical that you involve your key team members in a more formal feedback mechanism. Perhaps consider using a Team Advisory Board (TAB) strategy to get to the bottom of issues or suggestions for improvement.

A TAB gives you insight into those things about your business that make good people want to work with you, as well as those things that your team members find frustrating.

You will find that your team members have powerful ideas about how you could very quickly put new systems into place that would positively affect productivity and profitability. As the people on the front line, they often know how best to do it.

Remember, the objective of the meeting is not to engage in a complaint session. But if complaints arise, they are very useful information. More often than not, unhappy team members are not the source of a problem in a company – collective dissatisfaction is likely the result or symptom of problems within an organisation!

Whenever we have a new team member join, it is so important that we share our views on the type of the culture we have built and emphasise the importance of teamwork to generate the

CHAPTER 6: THE SECOND WAY – INCREASE THE NUMBER OF TIMES CUSTOMERS COME BACK

results of impacting the lives of the families of our customers, our local community and the lives of those less fortunate around the world.

When looking at the value of teamwork I remember a valuable analogy that was taught at the Accountant's Boot Camp, that I attended way back in 1999!

That analogy related to the fascinating and extensive studies undertaken by wildlife scientists studying geese and other migratory birds always fly in a distinctive v-formation.

Here are some of the interesting findings:

As each goose flaps its wings, it creates uplift for the birds that follow. By flying in a "V" formation, the whole flock adds 70% extra flying range.

People who share a sense of community can help each other get where they are going more easily... because they are travelling on the trust of one another. When people work together harmoniously on teams, sharing common values and a common destination, they all arrive at the destination quicker and easier, because they are lifted up by the energy and enthusiasm of one another.

When a goose falls out of formation, it suddenly feels drag and resistance flying alone. It quickly moves back to take advantage of the lifting power of the birds in front. Consequently, when the lead goose gets tired, it drops out of the front position and moves to the rear of the formation, where the resistance is lightest, and another goose moves to the leadership position. This rotation of position happens many times in the course of the long journey to warmer climates.

If we have as much sense as geese, we stay in formation with those headed where we want to go. We are willing to accept their help and give our help to others. When a team is functioning well, various members of the team may take the leadership role for a while because of a particular expertise or experience. Consequently, on good teams, everyone has the opportunity to serve as a leader as well as a follower.

- **Geese rotate leadership**. When the lead goose tires, it drops back into the formation and another goose flies to the point position.

It pays to take turns doing the hard tasks. We should respect and protect each other's unique arrangements of skills, capabilities, talents, and resources. When a team is functioning well, various members of the team may take the leadership role for a while because of a particular expertise or experience. Consequently, on good teams, everyone has the opportunity to serve as a leader as well as a follower.

- **Geese honk at each other.** The geese flying in formation HONK to encourage those up front to keep up with their speed.

  We need to make sure our HONKING is encouraging. In groups where there is encouragement, production and team output is much greater. Individual empowerment results from quality honking. Similarly, when working on teams, it is exceedingly important for each team member to communicate regularly with all the other team members. Teams frequently fall apart because of the lack of adequate communication among the various members of the team. Perhaps human teams can learn from flying flocks of geese that constant communication among members is exceedingly important in moving effectively towards a common destination.

- **Geese help each other.** Scientists also discovered that when one goose becomes ill, is shot or injured, and drops out of the formation, two other geese will fall out of formation and remain with the weakened goose. They will stay with and protect the injured goose from predators until it is able to fly again or dies. Likewise, human teams work best when they do more than just work together, but care for the wellbeing of each other.

Teamwork involves caring, sharing and working together to achieve a common goal, purpose or result.

We would all look like silly 'gooses' if we did not imitate nature to some degree – don't you agree?

The value of newsletters, blogs and 'community' groups

I love writing blogs and newsletters because they are another great tool to get your customers coming back to your business over and over. One word of warning though, your content shouldn't be just another piece of marketing 'blurb.'

This kind of writing is all 'us, us, us' and is merely designed to blow the company's own trumpet without giving anything of real value.

It's vital to focus your blog/newsletter in on the customers' needs and answer the question 'What's In It – For Me?' from the customers' perspective.

If you do that, your customers will look forward to every issue.

Make your blog/newsletter interesting by offering news; hints and tips; how-to's; guest column writers; offers; latest stories and articles

CHAPTER 6: THE SECOND WAY – INCREASE THE NUMBER OF TIMES CUSTOMERS COME BACK

contributed by specialists, team members, industry professionals, and even customers. (Images/Photographs are good, too!).

Your blog/newsletter needs to add value.

It must help the readers in some way.

Ask them this question "if you had a magic wand and you wanted to fix a niggling issue in relation to the products/services we sell, what would you wish for?"

Help them remove the things that 'keep them awake at night' or answer queries that regularly come up in conversations or telephone calls.

Adding value is one the easiest and most cost-effective ways to nurture your customers and make sure they keep coming back to your business. For example, you could add value by gifting them 'soft dollar' products or services. That is, items that have a high perceived value in the customers' eyes and a low hard dollar cost to you.

You could send them special reports or make your customers feel special with advance-notice events or a hotline service that goes above and beyond the industry standard.

You can use offers, vouchers, and special invitations to reactivate old customers, or you could establish a loyalty program right from the start. Here, every customer is given an incentive to continue to come back and purchase from the business.

For instance, a business loyalty card could be stamped every time they buy something. After a certain number of stamps, they might receive something for free.

Or you could develop a 'customer club' or Facebook community group that offered certain advantages to regular customers, like special promotions, front row seats to events in a VIP area or other privileges.

Classify your customers in value segments

Another way to make sure the right customers keep on coming back is to classify your customer base into A, B, C, and D customers.

'A' class customers would be your best customers, B customers have the potential to become A's, C customers are not ideal, and D customers might be referred to your competitors!

This classification process means that your ongoing communication and promotions to these various types of customers will be more appropriate for each group.

Here, only your 'A' customers might be invited to join your 'customer club,' for example.

Nurturing your customers from the very first phone call, through to thanking, offering guarantees, and reassuring them after their purchase can help you avoid post-purchase dissonance. ('Post-purchase dissonance' means that someone takes goods home or purchases services from your business and then regrets it.) In fact, you can attract those customers back to your business.

The same can be said if you have some specific techniques to turn complaints into praise. This can be done by establishing policies about how to look after unhappy customers. You and your team should agree to do everything possible to turn that customer around.

One way to do this and to avoid this kind of issue in the first place is to always ask for feedback from your customers.

Asking for feedback makes them think you're truly interested in them and, as such, makes them come back to you more freely.

You will come to mind before anyone else, largely because you bothered to ask their opinion!

Often, your competitors won't ever have bothered and so your customers will be suitably impressed.

Aside from this, people just like to be asked because it is human nature and more often than not, they like to help!

The Power of Customer Advisory Boards

Customer Advisory Boards – where you invite groups of customers to talk about the service they received, what could be improved, and feedback forms – can be useful tools here.

Imagine one of your customers sitting down at a luncheon with several other business owners. The subject of your business comes up.

What will your customer say about you and your business?

Will it be positive?

Will it be negative?

Or worse yet, will it be nothing at all?

Will your customer, instead, be silent, listening carefully to what's being said by others while internally running down a list of comparisons of your business vs. your competition being discussed?

It's a given that customers are thinking about you and the service your business provides. Even if they aren't talking about you to other business owners, they're evaluating your business every time you provide a your product or service. They're also evaluating your firm every time you answer the phone, return a call, or send out an invoice or other correspondence.

Ironically, it's often the non-technical aspects of what you do that are noticed most by customers. We know that customers often don't return not because the business was technically incompetent, but because of the way they were treated.

It comes down to the issue of perceived indifference. You know, the little things that communicate to the customer that they aren't as important to the business as they think they should be.

What are your business's areas of perceived indifference?

Your phone procedures?

Your billing procedures?

The way you deliver your product or service?

The amount of contact with your customers?

The attitude of a team member?

Accessibility?

Timeliness?

How about the incessant sound of the same Christmas Carols being played every day during the Christmas period each day, each year – yes, this was a real one from a recent CAB we ran for a customer!

Whatever your issues of perceived indifference, you owe it to yourself to find out what they are and fix them – now!

Every day you wait, you risk losing a customer who feels unheard or uncared for.

So, how do you determine your issues?

We've found the best way to reveal what those issues are is to ask.

Here's the really important part: you must really listen to your customers. They already have the answers and are more than willing to share them.

Hold a Customer Advisory Board—ASAP!

And remember, *"It's the little things that make you stand out from your competitors."*

Chasers Tip   Invest in a CRM to keep close to your customers.

Chapter 7

The Third Way – Increase Your Average Sale of Each Sale

This third way is designed to give you insight into the increase in your business that could simply be achieved by selling an extra item or two with the customer's original purchase!

Increasing your average sale means tapping into a sales opportunity already sitting right there in front of you. An opportunity that could add value to your customers and could increase that purchase and grow your business to boot!

Most business owners focus their marketing energy on winning customers. However, getting your customers to come back to your business more often is vital to the long-term health and profitability of your business.

As is increasing your average sale!

And that's what you'll learn more about in this chapter.

You see, people often won't know or won't think about other items or services that might add to the first product or

CHAPTER 7: THE THIRD WAY – INCREASE YOUR AVERAGE SALE OF EACH SALE

service they intend to purchase and so they'll need you to make suggestions.

Suggestions that would increase the average sale for your business.

After all, customers come to you for help and guidance. It's important, then, to let them know about all their options, including additional services or products that can add to their original purchase.

Every time you fail to do that, it's a sales opportunity gone begging!

You paid good money to get that phone to ring or that customer to inquire. It's important to make the most the effort for your customers and your business. And most businesses frequently let the customer come in, select what they want, and leave.

Many do so without making any suggestions about what might add to the original purchase.

In fact, increasing your average sale makes that transaction all the more profitable.

You see, the cost of winning that new customer was already covered in the original purchase item.

Anything over and above this is a plus – profit for you!

So what is your 'average sale' or 'average transaction value'?

Simply, it is total value of sales divided by the number of customers you dealt with.

For example:

You might have turned over $4,286 in the last week. On checking your records, like your order book or the number of transactions recorded for the week on your register, you might have sold to 62 customers.

This would mean $4,286 divided by 62 is your average sale for that week. So approximately $69.13 is the average sale.

Consider for a moment what happens to that weekly sales figure if, by better merchandising or cross-selling additional items, for example, you could increase that figure to $74.60. That's only an additional $5.47 to each customer, not much by any stretch of the imagination. And yet it takes your weekly turnover from $4,286 to $4,625.50.

Now, this difference ($339.50 per week) might not seem like much of a difference or anything to make a big song and dance about, but think again.

Calculate that difference – $339.50 by 52 weeks – and it's nothing to sneeze at!

Go ahead and do that now. In this example alone, it means an additional $17,654 in turnover. Who knows what it could mean for your business!

This is even more important when you consider that $17,654 is almost entirely profit.

You paid to get the customer to your business anyway and you already had the team to serve them for their original inquiry, so the only additional cost is the hard cost to you of delivering the extra product or service sold at the same time as the sale for the original purchase! Making that additional figure – just $5.47 and $17,654 – a very profitable addition indeed!

Once again, there are many, many ways to get your customers to spend more when they deal with you.

CHAPTER 7: THE THIRD WAY – INCREASE YOUR AVERAGE SALE OF EACH SALE

Some easy ways to increase your average sale

Often the best place to start when it comes to increasing the average transaction value is to identify 'cross-selling' opportunities.

Cross-selling occurs when you sell other products or services from your product or service range in addition to your customer's initial inquiry. Suggestive selling is another term often used here, that is, an additional item or service is suggested to the customer at the time of sale.

To help you create cross-selling opportunities in your business, go to every major product or service and ask:

'What else can we offer the customer to go with this purchase?'

'What else could we offer that would add value and make the use of this product or service better?'

'What else, when coupled with this product or service, would help them get the most out of it?'

From here you can create 'cross-selling checklists' for each item. These checklists would give your team members guidance about what best to suggest to customers.

It should also become compulsory, a performance standard for every single sale.

We all know of McDonald's or the 'Big Mac' which is a favourite fast food of most kids these days (including mine when they were very young – probably not so much these days though!) Well, McDonald's have a performance standard for every sale down to a fine art – they really do – so much so that it has become the catch cry of any business looking to implement a similar system.

For instance, McDonald's make a point of cross-selling every single time, don't they?

They ask, 'Would you like fries or a drink with that?'

Or 'Would you like an apple pie with your burger?'

McDonald's knows full well the financial value of cross-selling and is not about to take any chances. So much so that if a team member fails to cross-sell 3 times within the same shift, they're reprimanded, retrained, or in some cases fired!

When the young salesperson at McDonalds asks, 'Would you like some french fries with that?'—that's a cross-selling system in action.

This information is designed to give you insight into what cross-selling could do for your business.

You see, cross-selling—selling other items from 'across' your range at the same time as the customers make their initial purchase—is a vital concept. It's a selling style that contributes greatly to the third way to grow your business, that is, to increase your average sale.

Most business owners focus their marketing energy on winning customers. Getting customers to come back more often is vital to the long-term health and profitability of your business.

By understanding this issue, you could add more value to your customers and increase your profitability.

Often the best place to start when it comes to increasing the average transaction value is to identify 'cross-selling' opportunities. So let's do that now.

Cross-selling occurs when you sell other products or services from across your product or service range in addition to your

CHAPTER 7: THE THIRD WAY – INCREASE YOUR AVERAGE SALE OF EACH SALE

customer's initial inquiry. Suggestive selling is another term often used here; that is, an additional item or service is suggested to the customer at the time of sale.

You know that if someone buys a product or service from you, they probably also need another product or service. So make sure you ask them, each and every time.

To help you create cross-selling opportunities within your business, go over every major product or service with your team and ask:

'What else can we offer the customer to go with this purchase?'

'What else could we offer that would add value and make the use of this product or service better?'

'What else, when coupled with this product or service, would help them get the most out of it?'

Or write a list of popular sale items, then brainstorm a list of companion items you could sell with these products or services.

From here, you can create 'cross-selling checklists' for each item. These checklists would give your team members guidance as to what best to suggest to customers.

It could literally be a checklist that your team member and your customers could work through together. Or for your team members alone.

And together you'll create a checklist they'll be happy to use because they helped create it. These lists could also be hung in various areas, or they could be reprinted on invoices or 'shelf talkers.'

You could have your team members present the checklist to customers after they've decided on their purchase.

'So that we can help you best, is it okay if we run through a quick checklist just to make sure we've covered everything you need?'

Most customers will say 'yes' because positioning it this way means the customers can see a benefit in doing so.

Another idea: Focus on cross-selling just one item every month or week. For example, you could offer a 'monthly or weekly special' to every single customer every time for that month.

This item would be one of your 'what everybody needs' type of products or services. Offer it with every purchase. Your team can feel comfortable asking this question because, in effect, they might be saving the customer money.

If the customer says no, it doesn't matter. You already have a sale in any case. And if customers do say no, you still know you've given them a better service by asking if they need anything else.

As the customer is about to purchase, you could suggest an item in this way:

'Just before you go, there's something you might be interested in. You see, this month's special is [product or service type]. It's a great special because [offer benefits, such as price saving or advantages]. Shall I include that for you, too?'

Many people will find it easier to say yes than no. This is particularly true if the item has a low dollar cost.

As you saw before, you don't really need to increase *each* sale by much to have it significantly affect your profitability.

Because of that, you could offer every customer a low dollar item special.

CHAPTER 7: THE THIRD WAY – INCREASE YOUR AVERAGE SALE OF EACH SALE

In doing so, because the item might actually be a small one, you would use the script just detailed AND the suggested actions that follow.

For example, you might have tallied up their purchases, rung them up, and bagged all the items. Before you total it, say the script outlined above, while holding the bag in one hand and the low dollar special item in the other, over the bag itself.

This makes it even easier for the customer to say yes.

And if you know the item is a good one, that'll be of some value, you can feel confident that this is adding value and truly offering service.

Some people feel that adding on products or services to a sale is being a bit 'pushy.' However, it's vital to understand that you can only truly serve your customers if you fulfil their needs and delight them with the outcome of their purchase. Bringing a product or service home and having it not perform as they'd hoped, or as it could have when combined with something else, doesn't fulfil that need.

For example, you have the flu, go to a pharmacy, and walk out with some aspirin and a box of tissues. You've taken a cheap solution, but it's far from the best one for you. The pharmacist could have helped more by selling you a remedy, like cough medicine.

If you educate your team members that they are, in fact, providing a service for the customers by reminding or informing them, then implementation of cross-selling will happen more easily.

So to have your team feeling more and more comfortable with cross-selling, it's a good idea to educate them, using this information, involving them in the development of the cross-selling checklists, and so on.

Further, it's sometimes a good idea to offer your team members incentives or to have a little competition among themselves. For example, you could create a form like the one below:

Team Member	Items Cross-Sold	Value $
Josie Stephens	Shoe polish and shoe laces	$8.65
Bev Evans	A second pair of shoes in a different colour, shoe polish	$62.00

Every time a team member cross-sells an item, they write it up on the form. At the end of the week, the results are tallied up and the highest cross-seller wins a prize, like movie tickets, a morning off, or dinner for 2.

Imagine what a difference that would make! Better yet, imagine what a difference it would make if your team member actually had a checklist to run through with the customer. As mentioned earlier, the checklist could be a sign hanging from the ceiling or a shelf talker.

Consider this example happening EVERY SINGLE time a customer walks into the local fuel convenience store.

This business added tens of thousands of dollars to its net profit by simply asking every person who came in to pay for fuel:

'Just a friendly reminder: Do you have enough bread and milk?'

This was done in a friendly way and really did help people. There's nothing worse than getting home and remembering you've forgotten to pick up the basics. A significant percentage of people bought the bread or milk.

It's also important to note that these items would otherwise have been purchased elsewhere if the customer hadn't been reminded.

It really can be that simple: ask and you shall receive. The question is, how could you ask for that added sale for your business?

Three Levels of pricing

Another way to increase your average sale is to upsell inquirers from, for example, the budget item to the middle-priced item.

One great way to do that is to offer your products or services in 3 or more tiers, along the lines of 'good,' 'better,' and 'best,' or 'gold,' 'silver,' and 'bronze.'

Your 'good' product or service might actually be your budget product or service, the one for the price-conscious buyer. The one you offer when you discount (hopefully very rarely is this one purchased!)

Your 'better' product or service is the one you actually want the majority of people to buy, This one is more valuable than the 'bronze,' would include additional value-added features, accessories, or additions.

And your 'best' will appeal to those who are happy to spend a little more for a lot more – the most valuable product/service you offer. It comes with the most additional features and services, like laser shows, pyrotechnics, the whole 'kit and caboodle'!

Or, if you have a broad range of products or services, always make a recommendation on 3 that could suit. Then go through and explain that the first is good, the second is better and probably ideal, and the third is the best in that range.

Statistics show most people will select the item in the middle...

... and by doing so you have just increased the average value of the sale!

Package together your products or services

As with 'cross-selling,' when it comes to increasing the average transaction value, one of the best places to start is to identify 'packaging' opportunities.

In the first instance, it needs to be noted that several packaging options are available to you, depending on your business.

First, you could package products and products together. Second, services and services together. And finally, products and services together. This can happen in several ways, all of which are designed to make your products and services more attractive, add value to the customers, and increase your average sale.

You know that if someone buys a product or service from you, they probably also need another product or service, so the idea here is to package these items together in the first place.

One option is to identify those items your customers really do need to make the most of the original product or service that interested them. These would be 'companion items'—items that 'match' the product or service and actually allow the customer to

CHAPTER 7: THE THIRD WAY – INCREASE YOUR AVERAGE SALE OF EACH SALE

enjoy more benefits or gain more use or value from the product or service.

These items could be 'bundled' with the main item to create a whole package that is more attractive than the individual parts. This increases the value of the sale.

In packaging items or services together – that is bundling them into one single purchase – usually you add value to the customer.

For example, an electrical retailer might offer a free TV wall bracket to hang the new TV on with any purchase of a new LCD TV. Instead of discounting the price by 20% with any purchase, a manufacturer might offer installation valued at $245. Or a health professional service-based business might package together a health assessment and 8 sessions for the price of 6. All this is designed to make your products and services more attractive and to add value to the customers.

Better yet, your average sale will increase.

Another example would be to create whole 'kits,' including everything a person needs to do the task or enjoy the product purchased.

Another would be special-occasion packages based around events in the yearly calendar, like Mother's Day, Father's Day, Christmas, Easter, Valentine's Day, the official day for the celebration of the country or state, and so on.

For example, if you own a delicatessen, you could put together a full 'Christmas Pudding Pack' and promote making puddings at home. This pack could include a fabulous Christmas Pudding recipe and all the delicious ingredients for a price that is better value overall but that still increases your average sale.

A manufacturer of condiments or flavourings, which sells to restaurants and commercial kitchens, could package together 3 complimentary items.

If you own a pharmacy, you could package a whole range of items into a first-aid kit, including bandages, antiseptics, a booklet on treating common injuries, and so on. Or you could create a 'Mother's Day Delight' package that includes items that pamper Mum—perfume, powder, bath oils, makeup, and so on.

McDonald's gives us plenty of packaging examples. You've probably seen and even purchased and eaten their 'Value Meal Deals,' where a burger, drink, fries, and dessert are packaged together. They win because their average transaction goes through the roof, and the customers win because the total price paid is less than the total cost of the individual items.

Remember too, that these add-on items, packaged together, are often high-margin items, thus adding significantly to the profit per transaction, too.

If you are a serviced-based business, you can package one service with another that's complementary, just as these examples have shown. The difference is simply that you replace products with services!

You could package certain services with others that will help your customers get greater value out of the first service.

A service-based business, such as a health professional, might package together a health assessment and 8 sessions for the price of 6. For example, a physiotherapist or masseuse could package together a number of sessions, say 6, and call it the 'Getting Better'

CHAPTER 7: THE THIRD WAY – INCREASE YOUR AVERAGE SALE OF EACH SALE

pack (meaning 'getting better for money as well'). By pre-purchasing the 'Getting Better' sessions, they'll save 15% or receive their last session for free. (If this increases the average number of sessions from 4 to 6, then you've increased not only the average sale, but also the number of times customers deal with you.)

A dentist could package together tooth care products into an 'Improve Your Smile' pack.

A lawyer could package together a 'Legal Risk Analysis' with a common service, such as completing wills or property deeds.

You could package in a follow-up service to go with the professional service, thereby increasing your average sale and the service your customers receive. In this way, kits could be an option as well.

You could also bonus in special reports, for example, 'When you begin this service before March 12, you'll receive 3 bonus reports on how to this, that, and the other thing, valued at $49.95 each. This is a bonus to you valued at $149.85, so call 1800-555555 now. Remember you must book before March 12 to get those excellent reports free and save $149.85. CALL NOW!'

Including educational information about your products, services, or business as part of the package could build customer confidence in you and so increase the sale value, too. As could having various sales tools on hand, like a list of testimonials from happy customers, references, the '6 questions' test (mentioned earlier in Chapter 2, and illustrated by way of an example at Appendix 4, and more.

If you offer both products and services, these ideas can be applied here to package the two together. You could create kits that include products and services, for example. Further, in a price-competitive industry, this can be a particularly good way to differentiate yourself.

For example, let's say you manufacture residential venetian blinds. If you have ever shopped for that kind of product, you'd probably agree that it's a price-competitive industry. The majority of businesses discount to win business!

Now, let's imagine you packaged a product and a service together. So what could you do instead of discounting? *(Because discounting kills your profits and gets little response from customers!)* Offer something that probably has a lower hard cost to you. Something like a service. A service such as the installation of those blinds.

So rather than discounting the price by 20% to win new business, the offer could be to 'Invest in Best Value Blinds & Curtains for your home and you'll enjoy a hassle-free, professional installation, normally valued at $385 – absolutely free!'

This makes it easy for your customers to differentiate you from your competitors on something other than price! It also means you're saving your bottom line. And because a professional installation makes your customer's life easier, you'd be adding more value to your customers, too!

To help you create packaging opportunities within your business, work with your team and go through every major product or service with this in mind:

'What else can we offer the customer to go with this purchase?'

'What else could we offer that would add value and make the use of this product or service better?'

'What else, when coupled with this product or service, would help them get the most out of it?'

Or write a list of popular sale items, then brainstorm a list of companion items you could sell with these products or services.

Educating your customer to buy

Following on from that, merchandising can also increase your average sale. Signage, ticketing, presentation, and packaging; establishing particular sales points within the premises; mapping out (walking) traffic flow through stores; and having some easy-to-sell items by the register or your office can be other great merchandising ploys to increase your average sale.

Having educational information about your products, services, or business available to your customers could build their confidence in you and so increase the sale value. As could having various sales tools on hand, like a list of testimonials from happy customers, references, the '6 questions' test, and more.

In fact, it's a great idea to develop a sales system. That is, a way of selling that constantly involves cross-selling, upselling, and packaging. In this way, you know that every single team member is following the same system.

Surprisingly, on-hold messages about your business can spark a customer's interest in something else you do and as such increase the average sale. For example, imagine calling a business about a specific product or service. Unfortunately, you're put on hold for a moment, but you learn about other products or services offered by the business. Products or services you may not otherwise have known about.

Margins and Prices

And finally, the all-important issues of margins and price.

To increase your average sale, you must have a full grip on your margins and what they really mean to your back pocket. Avoiding discounting and price wars is all-important to maintain and increase your average sale.

Consider these facts uncovered by extensive research and you will have to agree.

If your present margin is 35% and you reduce your prices by 10%, to produce the same profit as you would have BEFORE the discount, your sales volume must increase by a staggering 40%. That's not to make any more money, only to get back to where you were BEFORE you offered the discount!

And let's face it, a measly 10% discount isn't going to excite an extra 40% in sales, is it?

Have a look at the Margin Tables in Appendix 6.

Conversely, if your present margin is 35% and you increased your prices by 10%, your sales may reduce by up to as much as 22% to produce the same profit. Chances are this simply wouldn't be the case, either.

Let's explore why a little further.

CHAPTER 7: THE THIRD WAY – INCREASE YOUR AVERAGE SALE OF EACH SALE

If your business provides better quality advice and products or more detailed services than competitors, it's not apples for apples, is it?

This means you may be able to entertain the thought of increasing some of your prices. It's your higher level of servicing over a lower level available from competitors. Most times, people only shop on price because it's been how we've been trained to find what we want.

Statistics show only 15% of the market actually purchase on the basis of price.

Oddly enough, sales can sometimes increase with a price increase. Your products or services seem more valuable all of a sudden!

This is particularly true if you create sales and marketing tools to educate customers about the value they'll receive.

Price versus value and service

The issue of price versus value and service has been a hot topic practically from the day trade and commerce began. Because of this, many studies have been completed to analyse exactly why customers buy.

In the search for some answers, one such survey has looked, perhaps more importantly, at why customers *don't* buy from you or why they leave you and move to a competitor.

People were asked this question:

> 'Why do you choose not to deal with a business or to leave a business and go to a competitor?'

The results time and again have been astounding. For your interest they were:

Convenience	3%
Relationship at a high level	9%
Miscellaneou	5%
Product/price/time	15%
'Perceived indifference'	68%
	100%

The 'convenience' category means a person would choose not to deal with a business or would leave that business because it's more convenient to purchase elsewhere.

'Relationship at a high level' means, for example, a person close to you opened a new business or moved to another company and you want to continue dealing with that person. It could be a relative or a close friend or someone you held in very high regard.

'Miscellaneous' is simply those reasons that couldn't be categorised clearly.

'Product/price/time' actually means potential customers want a certain product or service, at a certain price, whenever they want it—for example, right now, next week, or what have you. For argument's sake, let's just say this category is price, so this group represents people who buy or don't buy on the basis of price.

CHAPTER 7: THE THIRD WAY – INCREASE YOUR AVERAGE SALE OF EACH SALE

'Perceived indifference' is literally that. Your customers or potential customers feel you or your team members are *indifferent* toward them. Indifferent meaning they're given the impression you couldn't care less if they purchased from you or not.

This means virtually 7 out of 10 inquiries (you don't sell to) walk away because they feel your business is indifferent toward them compared to only 15% of customers who shop on price alone.

Seven out of 10 inquirers who fail to purchase from you are doing so because they felt your business didn't care enough, didn't take time for them, and really didn't make a difference!

That's just amazing, especially when you consider that ONLY 15% of the market shop or purchase on price alone.

And yet this 15%, or the price-sensitive group, are usually the ones most businesses incorrectly pay the greatest attention to.

It's obvious that some industries are more price-sensitive than others and these results may therefore vary for your business. But it's critical to remember that surveys have been completed the world over, in every walk of life. As such, it's vital to understand that the vast majority of people really do purchase along these lines.

And the fact is, even if you feel these results may only be partially true for your business, you'll still be facing an opportunity to INCREASE sales. An interesting idea but...

... sometimes, it just doesn't feel true though, right?

Even though these statistics will most likely prove true for your business as well, there are some good reasons why business owners, managers, and team members alike might feel price truly is a big issue.

Let's look at some of those now.

First, what do most businesses promote? Most focus on promoting the features of the product or service and then—the almighty price!

Usually, what that product or service can actually 'do' for the customer, that is, the benefits it might bring, are ignored. In fact, very often price becomes the focus of advertising or marketing material. So in fact, we as business owners and managers literally train our customers to shop on price by displaying a product or service and the price over and over again.

Product...price.
Service...price.
Product...price.
Service...price.

Most marketing material fails to explain the benefits to the customers—what this product or service could mean to their life, their business, their home, their children, their car, or any number of factors relating to that purchase—and so places the emphasis back on price.

Or your industry *might* actually be heavily price-competitive. Make no bones about it, there are some areas that suffer more than others; however, there are almost always ways to combat this problem.

Or you might have the kind of business where either, over the phone or face-to-face, an inquiry starts with 'How-much-is-it?' Or 'I want to find out the price of an XYZ,' 'Could you tell me the price of...?' Or a similar phrase that makes it sound like the caller or visitor is just shopping for price.

CHAPTER 7: THE THIRD WAY – INCREASE YOUR AVERAGE SALE OF EACH SALE

Now think about what most businesses say when asked that sort of question.

That's right.

The price!

For example, 'OK, that'd be $40, $400, or $4,000,' whatever the price actually is. Sure enough, many potential customers (the potential customer you've paid to have call or visit you through your advertising costs) then say, 'Thanks very much. I'll get back to you.'

Mostly, they never do. They call 2 or 3 other suppliers of the same sort of product or service – your competitors – and ask the same question.

Unfortunately, your competitors do the same thing when they call – give them the price and let them go.

And here's the crunch. At that point, would your potential customers have *anything else* to judge you by *except for price?*

Frankly, no!

And most business owners complain about people who shop on price alone! If your business handles price inquiries this way, you couldn't possibly expect your customers to do anything but!

In this example, you've given them no reason other than price to choose you or a competitor.

Clearly, they've indicated they're interested in your product or service by calling you in the first place.

In this instance, the business has failed to take the customer's cue. You see, most people only ask about price as a place to *start*, yet most businesses assume this question is the start *and* finish.

To add to that, you haven't given them any reason to believe you *aren't* indifferent toward them. In fact, it would appear you are indeed like everyone else.

If most people only ask about price as a place to start and then, from the customer's point of view, nobody bothers to ask what they want the product or service for or to do for them, you could see how someone might think you're being indifferent toward them.

Nobody asked what they were really after—what type, colour, number, make they wanted, when they would need it by, or how they wanted to pay for that, and more. Plus, the business lets the customer get off the phone without capturing any follow-up details.

All of these points are critical because these or similar points offer you a great, easy, and cost-effective way to stand out from the crowd!

Focusing on customer service, improving what it is you do, doing something out of the ordinary or different – something totally unexpected from your industry, and offering genuine advice on how a product or service will make a difference in a customer's life – rather than just price – will increase your sales.

The interesting statistics – 7 out of 10 people won't buy from you because of 'perceived indifference' rather than price – show that a happy potential customer will buy regardless.

You see, customers who feel they've been served well, received value for money, and got good service will often buy a product or service without overly considering the price. These customers feel service and quality is more important. And when you offer better service, customers will not only buy at a higher price, they will often

CHAPTER 7: THE THIRD WAY – INCREASE YOUR AVERAGE SALE OF EACH SALE

talk favourably to others about your business and your products and services, pay less attention to your competitors and their advertising, and may well buy other products and services from your business.

The key to a happy customer is customer service. Not just service but 'awesome service.' To differentiate your business or have people pay a higher price, service that delights is what you need to offer.

Another awesome tip is to provide the price way up front in your *'Proposals'* (note the word 'quote' was not used here nor anywhere else anymore and you'll know why if you are fully taking in the information in this book!) and then follow it with *'and this includes a number of very special things'*, which you highlight from the research you have conducted on the differences between you and your competitors!

This will help refocus your customer's attention from the actual price and shift it to the benefits of buying from you.

This way the focus is on the benefits of the product or service not the price which most business owners would leave at the bottom – and would be the last thing the customer focuses on and remembers! And hence starts the cycle of price shopping for the cheapest.

Whilst we are talking about prices consider how the display of the numbers on your promotions may impact your customer's decisions.

If you want to make a house look big, put a tent next to it.

If you want to make a house look small, put a skyscraper next to it.

That's the contrast effect at play, and it can work wonders for positioning your prices. If you want to make the price of the product you *want* to sell appear to be very small or reasonable, position a similar, but more expensive, product next to it.

In a now-classic study published in the *Journal of Marketing Research* and repeated in the Robert B Cialdini classic *Yes! 50 Scientifically Proven Ways to Be Persuasive,* Williams-Sonoma had a $275 bread maker listed in their print catalogue, and almost no one was buying it. When they introduced a similar bread maker for $429 and positioned it next to the $275 bread maker, sales of the $275 bread maker nearly *doubled*.

If you're in information marketing, creating that more expensive product is relatively easy; if you're a retailer or reseller, it can be a matter of bringing in those product lines or brands you've always believed to be too expensive for your customer base. The goal is not to sell the new expensive product – although wouldn't it be awesome if you did? – but rather to make the price of the original product look small, so you sell more of those.

For best results, try leading with the most expensive product.

This psychological behaviour is caused by a common cognitive bias called price anchoring – which refers to the tendency to heavily rely on the first piece of information offered when making decisions.

This is price anchoring at its most basic. It leverages a decision-making principle called primacy effect, where the first thing a person sees, especially in a list or lineup, sets their expectations for what follows. If the first price they see is very expensive, then they may be pleased to see the less expensive price that follows.

The order of the highest priced product to the lowest priced product can influence whether a customer chooses a product that is mid-ranged and therefore more profitable than the cheapest one merely because it is displayed.

CHAPTER 7: THE THIRD WAY – INCREASE YOUR AVERAGE SALE OF EACH SALE

So if you see a price that is higher at the top of, say a wine menu followed in consecutive prices down the list to the lowest, price anchoring suggests that most wine lovers will pick either the highest price or a mid-ranged one. Therefore, the simple re-arrangement of your prices can yield greater profits!

Obviously, increasing your price could be a great way to increase your average sale and could be worth further investigation for your business.

A 2009 study reported by Cornell University found that diners were more likely to spend more when the dollar sign was removed from the prices listed on the menu. Notably, this was a study of *diners reading menus*, but it's interesting nonetheless and worthy of trialling and testing if you're trying to make your high price more palatable.

Neiman Marcus doesn't use dollar signs when trying to sell their pricey items, like Valentino handbags. For an example of how to make a price appear smaller by dropping of the currency sign, check out:

https://www.neimanmarcus.com/en-au/c/designers-valentino-handbags-cat6410731

Another study, discussed here, found that a sale price is more palatable when it is written in a smaller typeface. A price that is physically large may create a perception of being "more." After all, things that are big are big; things that are small are small. Big prices should be big; small prices should be small.

We take the focus off the price of our services by keeping the font size small and by positioning the price away from the factors that users should be more concerned with, such as identifying the right service (plan) type and selecting the items required:

Red Tape

We take care of the annual tax headache, help free up your time on the paperwork, and spend time helping you grow your business.

- Xero Software
- Annual Financial Statements
- Income Tax Returns
- BAS Returns
- Tax Management Liason with the ATO
- Free brief phone calls and unlimited emails
- 1 meeting per year

From $400 month (excl GST)

If you want regular dashboard reporting and frequent conversations about growing your business - as well as sorting out the basic tax requirements.

- Xero Software
- Annual Financial Statements
- Income Tax Returns
- BAS Returns
- Tax Management Liason with the ATO
- Free brief phone calls and unlimited emails
- ASIC Annual Statement Lodgement
- Tax Planning Advice in April/May
- 4 meetings per year
- Management Report - Quarterly

From $550 month (excl GST)

Virtual CFO

For people who know the advantages of quality advice on a regular basis and want comprehensive reporting - leading to a larger business value!

- Xero Software
- Annual Financial Statements
- Income Tax Returns
- BAS Returns
- Tax Management Liason with the ATO
- Free brief phone calls and unlimited emails
- ASIC Annual Statement Lodgement
- Tax Planning Advice in April/May
- 6 meetings per year
- Management Reports - Monthly
- Annual Strategic Planning - One Page Plan'
- Annual Budget Cashflow and Re-forecasting
- 5 Year Plan to Increase Business Value

From $1,000 month (excl GST)

And never underestimate the power of subtracting a dollar or 3, also known as using "charm pricing." It may sound like psychological nonsense, but $19.99 continues to register as less expensive than $20, and $99 continues to register as more reasonable than $100.

Even better?

CHAPTER 7: THE THIRD WAY – INCREASE YOUR AVERAGE SALE OF EACH SALE

Use a 7 instead of a 9, as in $97 instead of $99.

Even on briefly reviewing these ideas, you may have discovered some ideas you may not have tried in your business. To really increase your average sale and grow this profit point for your business, it will be critical that you really learn, understand, and implement these ideas in full.

> **Chasers Tip** Experiment with these Pricing strategies and measure the results to see the impact they could have on your bottom line.

Chapter 8

The Fourth Way – Improve the 'Processes' within Your Business

This final way for growing your business is designed to give you an insight into the increase in your business that could be achieved by improving the processes within your business – the way you do what you do, whether it's serving customers, providing products or services, and so on.

To understand the strength gained by improving processes, consider that each time you do you are more likely to have a customer come back and spend more. And you're also more likely to generate new customers via referrals.

This is the last but definitely not the least way to grow your business.

It's this step that ties it all together.

Without it, it is very UNLIKELY that your business would achieve any of the first three.

Most business owners focus their marketing energy on winning customers. However, getting your customers to come back to your

CHAPTER 8: THE FOURTH WAY – IMPROVE THE 'PROCESSES' WITHIN YOUR BUSINESS

business more often is vital to the long-term health and profitability of your business. As is increasing your average sale!

To do all that, though, certain processes must exist within your business.

And that's what you'll learn more about here.

But in building an amazing business try to look for *moments of connection* in each of the processes you start to break down to improve. Develop the mind-set of 'is this how an inspiring business would do this?' when reviewing your processes and systems.

Once again, there are many, many ways to improve the processes in your business to win more customers, keep them coming back more often, and spend more each time. Here in this chapter you'll find just some of those key strategies to do just that.

Issues like improving the service offered to your customers, understanding the power of being polite, using thank you notes, having fun and helping your customers have fun, too, would all help you win more customers, keep them coming back, and increase your average sale.

However, without changing and improving some of the processes in your business, this simply won't happen.

Fully understanding and finding out whether your business is suffering from 'perceived indifference' – where you're losing nearly seven out of ten inquiries because prospective customers feel you're 'indifferent' toward them – is one level.

Changing the processes within your business – for example, the way a customer is greeted in the store, the way the phone is answered, and training your team to understand the effects of this phenomenon – is required to take it to the second level.

The step where it actually makes a difference to your sales!

When Ray Kroc founded McDonald's he had absolutely no intention of working behind a counter. In fact, he never even made a hamburger. He began with a different end in mind. He envisioned thousands of McDonald's stores around the world, each doing exactly the same thing in a predictable manner.

Knowing that, he knew he wouldn't be able to work *in* them, hence they would have to work *without* him! He then developed processes and systems structured around how to hire people, the colour the restaurants should be, the way a restaurant should be managed, right down to the way they should heat their buns. All of this occurred by having a vision, determining what needed to be done to get there and then carefully going over every little detail.

Contrast that with owners who run a typical hamburger place, like our local favourite – Kermonds Hamburgers – a world famous burger and listed as one of the things to do when visiting Australia in a national tourism magazine!

They're doing it, doing it, doing it, every single day. And that's precisely because they didn't begin with the end in mind. They set up a business that depended on the owner doing everything.

Their only vision was of ordering the goods to make the hamburgers, doing the stock control, frying the fries, grilling the burgers, buttering the buns, wrapping it all up, ringing up the sale and hoping to make ends meet at the end of the day.

As Michael Gerber points out in his book *The E-Myth Revisited: Why Most Small Businesses Don't Work and What to Do About It*, it's a myth that most businesses are started by entrepreneurs. Gerber suggests that most businesses are actually started by a person suffering from an entrepreneurial seizure.

That is, instead of creating a business that works, we create a business that is *us*. A business that often becomes all-consuming.

And worse yet, when it all becomes too much, we sell our most precious asset for far less than it would have been worth if we had started with the end in mind.

But it doesn't have to be that way. There really is another path. Consider again the true purpose of your business. Once you get the thought processes of beginning with the end in mind going, the true purpose comes out. Isn't the purpose of a business to create life – a life full of meaning for you and for the people with whom you interact? To matter and create meaning, for your niche of followers who 'get' your meaning to buy from you and, in doing so, reward you and allow you then to make a contribution to better the lives of those less fortunate around the world.

That's the purpose for my business!

What happens when you get to the end when you know it's finally complete?

If you really can begin with the end in mind, and create a systemised way of getting there, then it means that the business must have an end point. That is, there must be a point when you can stand back and say, "Now it's finally done."

If at that point you decide to sell the business, you're handing over a business worth many times more than when you started, simply because you thought about and developed the systems that allow the business to function successfully without you.

And if you decide to stay involved in the business in some way, you know that it can function independently of you.

It's not your life.

You've developed a business that you're a part of.

Yet you're still apart from it.

Walt Disney tells the story of being asked by a child if he drew Mickey Mouse.

'I had to admit I do not draw anymore,' said Disney.

'Then do you think up all the jokes and stuff?' asked the child.

'No, I don't do that either,' admitted Disney.

Finally, the child looked at him and said, 'Mr. Disney, just what *do* you do?'

'Well, sometimes I think of myself as a little bee,' Disney explained. 'I go from one area of the studio to another and gather pollen and sort of stimulate everybody. I guess that's the job I do.'

The legacy (or the 'bits of pollen') that Disney left behind still exists today – and no doubt will for a long time to come.

He created systems and processes that resulted in an indelible *'way we do things here'* that includes empowered team members sharing a truly magic culture and passion for what they do, and millions of happy customers who come back again and again.

CHAPTER 8: THE FOURTH WAY – IMPROVE THE 'PROCESSES' WITHIN YOUR BUSINESS

Creating 'The Way We Do It Here'

An important step to start working *on* your business is to simply develop systems for everything. A number of things happen when you do this. First, *you* don't have to perform the process. Second, it empowers your team members to take on more responsibility. And third, when you systemise, you automatically develop what we call "the way we do it here."

A central theme in Gerber's *E-Myth* is that most businesses fail or never reach their full potential because their owners spend too much time doing the work that the business does, rather than managing and growing it. Creating a systemised way of doing things not only makes the business run in a totally predictable way, it also makes your business worth much more because it doesn't have to rely on *you* to operate.

Think about this concept by comparing the your local hamburger restaurant (for me, it's Kermonds Hamburgers in Warrnambool) to McDonald's.

In which company would you rather own shares?

McDonald's, most likely.

Why?

Because McDonald's makes better hamburgers?

Probably not (*most locals like me are biased but we do have national credibility on our side too!*)

You'd pick McDonald's shares because the company works like clockwork no matter which restaurant you visit. They all have completely systemised processes that make them consistently high quality and *very* successful.

Working **ON** not **IN**

'Working **ON** your business, not **IN** it' is another critical area. If you, as the business owner or manager, are stuck day in and day out handling the day-to-day operations of the business, the growth of that business will be slow.

Simply put, you won't have time to implement the ideas you'll discover here and improve the business.

By working **ON** your business and establishing processes to help you do that, you *will!*

A great place to fully appreciate this idea of working **ON** and not **IN**, is in Michael Gerber's best-selling book – *The E-Myth Revisited – Why Most Small Businesses Don't Work and What to Do About It.*

Working **ON** and not **IN** basically means you'll be able to step outside of the day-to-day activities of the business, look objectively at your business as a whole, and grow your business from there. You might set aside each Wednesday, for example, to focus on one area of the business that needs to be systemised, over the whole year you will have accumulated 52 new systems, processes or ways for doing things more consistently and efficiently!

Building a business that matters based on functions rather than people is important, too.

You see, most businesses are built around specific people rather than the jobs, or functions, those people perform. Changing your business to one that is focused on functions first and that slots the right people into those functions will help you grow your business.

Develop procedures manuals

Developing systems and manuals to map out specific tasks will also help you do that.

In the 1950's American engineer, Edward W. Demming (redesigner of the Post WWII Japanese car industry and also known as the father of quality evolution) completed a study showing that only four per cent of mistakes in business were due to human error.

That is, particular people making a mistake.

The other ninety-six per cent was due to a lack of systems!

You see, systems clearly spell out how to do every single task your business needs to complete to serve customers and make a profit.

As such, it's important they're developed and documented in manuals that can be used for training team members, delegating work, and using day to day.

These systems and manuals make it clear for every single team member what needs to be done and how, leaving you more time to develop the business.

By developing them in online tools like Google Sites, with cloud access, any one of your team, can access them anywhere anytime that there is an available internet connection.

Establishing new 'performance standards' – ideal standards of performance required to serve your customers face-to-face or over the phone, or to produce or deliver the product or service successfully and profitably – are vital!

Performance standards for your phone

In fact, these 'performance standards' truly set great companies apart from the average, everyday business. To put that another way, great companies, which started out just like yours, have 'a way of doing it here.' They've taken time and effort to develop something that says, 'This is how we do it here.' And by setting those standards for the team to work to and customers to expect, they've grown their businesses.

It's like being part of a great football team. Each team member wears the same colours, and certain standards are expected from the players. All of this forms part of 'the way we do it here' for the football team. These standards create a standard of play so that the team wins over and over.

It's the same for your business. Like in sport, these standards give your customers a level of consistency you just can't have without a system.

CHAPTER 8: THE FOURTH WAY – IMPROVE THE 'PROCESSES' WITHIN YOUR BUSINESS

When it comes to phone performance standards, this consistency and highly professional way of answering the phone builds customer confidence in you and your ability to deliver.

And it means that your customers and potential customers feel a level of continuity each and every time they deal with you.

It means, too, that every team member is playing from the 'same sheet of music,' everyone knows what everyone else is doing, and customers are continually treated not just identically, but well.

And better yet, it makes you stand out glaringly from your competitors.

Generally, your competitors will be the same as most other businesses out there—they don't have an actual system for handling phone calls. It's usually just bad luck if a potential customer catches the least skilled person on the day they call. It's bad luck if the phone rings off the hook to no avail. It's bad luck if the person who answers the phone is having a bad day and sounds hostile over the phone. It's bad luck if they just give the caller the price and let them hang up without gathering the caller's details. It's just bad luck if the customer decides not to purchase!

True?

No.

The way someone is handled over the phone has absolutely nothing to do with luck, does it?

In reality, it has everything to do with the *lack* of a system.

Because of this, most businesses simply DO NOT make a good first impression on the phone.

This could be costing you thousands and thousands in lost sales.

In fact, it could mean you're not getting the response you should from the hundreds or thousands of dollars you've invested to make that phone ring in the first place! And right now – at this moment – this *will* be costing you personally, through lost PROFITS.

You may already have some standards in place; however, you'd be surprised to find that some of the more traditional ways of answering the phone could be causing your business grief. Also, you may find that some, not all, of your team members are working to those standards.

Where this is true, people will only do the best they can, which may or may not be the best for your business or your customers. You can't necessarily expect your entire team to have the people and phone skills you might have. With a system, everybody has something to work to, a *minimum* standard to meet when serving customers or customers over the phone.

Think about the standards you have in place to answer the phone right now. What length of time do you allow to answer the phone? What do you say if someone wants to speak with a colleague or 'the boss'? How do you take messages? Do you ask if you can help or do you just tell the caller that person is not here and leave it at that? Also think about any standards you might have for answering internal calls. How do you transfer calls? And so on.

Thinking about this, you may find that some team members use their first names only, others use their first name AND last name, whereas others will simply answer the phone by company name or department, for example: 'Accounts.'

CHAPTER 8: THE FOURTH WAY – IMPROVE THE 'PROCESSES' WITHIN YOUR BUSINESS

So you'll agree, the telephone is one of the main means of contact that customers and potential customers have with your business. It's important, then, that you treat them well, right from the very first conversation. Check out Appendix 7 – Performance Standards for your Phone for ideas on how you can develop a consistent, professional and helpful way to answer your phone every time.

What about a Collection System?

In Chapter Six, we discussed the positives in classifying your customers into value segments. Well, in improving the processes in your business to become more efficient, this classification also helps you quickly work out those customers that take a long time to pay.

Cash flow is probably the most important process of your business and you must get it right and continue to have one eye on it to survive and be successful. The amount of available cash your business has on hand at any given time provides an indication of your ability to operate on a day-to-day basis and meet obligations. Having a robust collection system is vital as this is the key part of the cash flow health of your business.

The more days (work in progress, stock or debtor days) that your business goes without cash, the longer it takes to you to pay your creditors and keep operations going. Check out Appendix 5 – Positive Cash Flow and Debtor Control for a quick refresher on these important fundamentals.

'Until further notice' agreements

An idea to improve debtors payments is to establish 'Until Further Notice' agreements, whereby you withdraw an agreed sum via direct debit until you receive further notice from the customer to end the arrangement.

This fee might be an ongoing service charge, monthly refills on a product, or any multitude of items. These arrangements make it easy for your customers to continue to buy from you.

What makes 'until further notice' agreements so useful is that your debtors consistently remain in control. With these arrangements, you don't have to chase the money; it's simply transferred from their account to yours every month like clockwork.

And your customers begin to forget they're paying. Because it comes out automatically, it just becomes one of their fixed monthly expenses, usually not one to be altered.

These are particularly valuable for steering poor paying customers that you are continually chasing for payment, into regular payers!

Complete your SWOT analysis

Likewise, understanding and addressing your 'strengths, weaknesses, opportunities, and threats' is important to your business development. It will also ensure that you maximise those strengths and opportunities to win more customers, keep them coming back, and spending more each time. And minimise any problem areas.

CHAPTER 8: THE FOURTH WAY – IMPROVE THE 'PROCESSES' WITHIN YOUR BUSINESS

Completing an analysis of your industry, your competitors, and market research could help you make sure your processes to achieve the first 3 ways to grow your business are better than your competitors.

And give you a leading edge.

In fact, measure your current operation performance, delivery record, customer happiness, and so on and ask this question:

'What is the one thing I could do in my business that is impossible to do, but would completely transform my business forever?'

You answer can help you build a competitive advantage in the processes within your business – and increase sales as a consequence.

Building an amazing business is all about moments of connection

We have learnt in the first way of growing a business that the costs of retaining existing customers tend to be much lower than those of acquiring new ones.

The success of this strategy ultimately depends on expanding the breadth and depth of customer relationships and on translating the resulting loyalty into higher sales of goods and services, as well as a healthier bottom line.

Although businesses can spend lots of money in traditional loyalty programs, in customer-relationship-management (CRM) technology, and in general service-quality improvements, most of these initiatives end in disappointment. According to Forrester research, only ten per cent of businesses surveyed strongly agreed that business results anticipated from implementing CRM were met or exceeded.

What's regularly missing is the moments of connection between the customer and frontline team members – the spark that helps transform wary or sceptical people into strong and committed brand followers. That moment of connection and the emotionally driven behaviour that creates it explain how great customer service companies earn trust and loyalty during those few interactions (for instance, a lost credit card, a cancelled flight/seat (remember the United Airlines public debacle with removing a passenger ahead of employee needs), a damaged piece of clothing, or investment advice) when customers invest a high amount of emotional energy in the outcome. Superior handling of these moments requires an instinctive frontline response that puts the customer's emotional needs ahead of the business's and the employee's agendas.

When breaking down the systems of a business into fine processes examine each process through the eyes of how an inspiring business would view and carry out that process. How can you delight your customer at each stage of what you do in your business?

The importance of team

Understanding why the word 'team' is so critical could improve the processes and your working environment dramatically. So much so

CHAPTER 8: THE FOURTH WAY – IMPROVE THE 'PROCESSES' WITHIN YOUR BUSINESS

that you could find yourself delegating more and more, giving you the free time you need to work **ON** your business rather than **IN** it.

Remember the geese analogy in Chapter 3?

Creating processes to help find and keep team members easily is valuable for the growth of your business too. If you don't have a means of sourcing new team members, qualifying them, and inducting them into your business, you'll struggle with growth, constantly trying to find the 'right people.'

So it is vital.

Training is another pivotal area for improving the processes within your business and as such achieving improvements in the first 3 areas. You see, building team member skills is the only way you can get them to change for the better within your business. Regardless of whether it's customer service, phone answering techniques, computer skills, or technical training, it will be extremely important to the ongoing development of your business.

Setting goals and completing a business plan can also ensure that your business develops in every area and that your processes improve.

Improving processes to control costs is also a key leverage point in generating more profit for you.

Even on briefly reviewing these ideas, you may have discovered some ideas you might not have tried in your business. To really increase your number of customers, the number of times they deal with your business, and your average sale, you must improve the processes within your business.

That way, you, your team, and your business will be able to implement new ideas in full and grow the profit for your business.

> **Chasers Tip** Look to create WOW moments for your customers with every interaction your business has with them.

Part Two

Seven major areas to help you win new customers

Section 1

Advertising & letter writing to help you win new customers

For years now, there have been two schools of thought about advertising. And it seems the two are diametrically opposed.

One suggests a focus on 'keeping your name in front of the customers. It suggests using 'plenty of white space' to make your ad look uncluttered. Pretty pictures and artistic graphics are good, too; and there must be catchy, clever copy to pique the reader's curiosity. (Often these ads won't even include a phone number to reach the company!)

This kind of advertising often focuses on the company itself (hence its name) or 'brand awareness' designed to make people recognise your business or your product or service brand. Generally, this kind of advertising might win awards but won't win the greatest award – an increase in sales.

It's known as 'institutional advertising'

Almost every print advertisement, mailing piece, radio, or television commercial you see is based on institutional, or image, advertising.

Institutional advertising seeks to create an image about your product, service, or company in the hope that people will remember you when they're ready to buy.

As such, these ads typically radiate 'buy from us because were wonderful.' Image advertising is almost always a complete waste of your marketing dollars. Why? Because it doesn't offer the reader tangible benefits and it doesn't ask for an immediate response.

Worse still, institutional advertising is expensive in that it virtually requires you to spend over a long period of time *before* you get any results. Even then, the results are practically impossible to measure.

At best, these ads produce deferred, long-term brand awareness. The problem is, most small – to medium-sized businesses, perhaps like your own, aren't a Nike or McDonald's and simply can't afford to market on brand power alone.

At worst, and this applies to ninety-five per cent of all the advertising you look at, institutional advertising is ineffective, a waste of your hard-earned marketing dollars, and it produces limited, if any, immediate results.

Most institutional advertising tells you how great the company paying for the advertising is, how old and stable they are, and so forth. It focuses on 'the institution,' the business itself.

But these are non-compelling points.

Why?

SECTION 1: ADVERTISING & LETTER WRITING TO HELP YOU WIN NEW CUSTOMERS

It would seem perfectly valid to focus on the company, let people know who you are, wouldn't it?

No.

Not in this format.

Simply because most customers don't care about those issues. What they really want to know is what your business can do for them, what benefits you can bring them. They ask, 'What's In It – For Me?' (WIIFM)

Institutional advertising just doesn't convey the answers to those sorts of questions. It fails to give reasons for the reader to favour your business over another. It looks great, but it doesn't make a strong case for the product or service you sell.

Further, it usually fails to direct the consumer to a buying decision. Some don't even include contact details, so even if potential customers liked the ad, they couldn't do anything about it!

As such, institutional advertising just won't get the results you're after.

This second school of thought focuses in particular on generating a 'direct response' from your advertising and marketing efforts. That is, getting someone to put their hand up when they read your ad, say, 'Yes, I'm interested,' and either ask for more information or buy right there and then.

Direct response advertising very often will get results

These types of ads focus on six other essential elements: a headline, a guarantee, offers, 'WIIFM?' body copy, a 'call to action,' and layout and design. These six elements are designed to do more than just project an image or a name. They educate your potential customers about your business or your products and services in a way that not only 'looks good' but also gets sales results.

Direct response advertising is, then, the exact opposite of institutional advertising. It is designed to evoke a reaction, an immediate response, action, visit, call, or purchasing decision from the viewer or reader.

This kind of ad is written from the customer's point of view.

It's all about the customer's needs rather than how great the company is. These direct response ads often look like an 'advertorial,' that is, an ad that looks and is written just like an editorial article in a newspaper.

You see, these days we live in the 'information age.' It follows that people crave information. So articles that look like news or provide value-added information like advertorials generate a better response than traditional institutional advertising that looks like an ad.

People don't read newspapers for advertisements – they read it for news, don't they?!

Interestingly, the highest rated television shows the world over are also news-related. So, the more your ad looks like news, the better the response for your business.

Further, most people these days are also better educated and therefore more discerning, so they expect to be given details.

Direct response advertising tells a complete story. It presents factual and specific reasons why your company, product, or service

SECTION 1: ADVERTISING & LETTER WRITING TO HELP YOU WIN NEW CUSTOMERS

is superior to all others and supports those claims with guarantees, testimonials, or statistics. It doesn't rely on mere conjecture (the 'just saying so' technique) used in a lot of institutional advertising.

Direct response advertising is much more effective than institutional advertising simply because consumer don't care about you or your motivations. All they care about is the benefit of your product or service. How will your product improve their situation and save them time, effort, and money? Why will your product or service improve their life?

By giving them the answers to these kinds of questions, you'll dramatically change the results of your advertising, which, in turn, will have a major impact on your bottom line.

This kind of advertising can also provide hints and tips about how to get the most out of the product or service or what to look for. That way, it adds value up front, making you an even more attractive supplier.

Direct response advertising is salesmanship in print or over the air. As salesmanship, it makes a complete case for the company, product, or service. It overcomes sales objections. It answers all major questions and promises performance or results.

It should give facts about the performance capabilities of your product or service. Tell about your risk-free warranty or money back guarantee. Give reasons why your product is superior to your competitors on a level that the consumer can understand and appreciate.

After you've built your case, tell the consumers precisely what action to take. Tell them how to reach you, find out more, call your business, what to look for, and who to ask for. Tell them what to do when the salesperson calls. Remind them of the risk-free purchasing arrangements and, most importantly, tell them what results they can expect by owning or using your product or service.

That's why a direct response ad directs people to action. It compels consumers to visit your establishment, call you, send in money, and so forth. It asks for the sale (the 'sale' can be an initial phone call or an outright purchase). Used effectively, direct response advertising can produce tons of super-qualified prospects who appreciate the information you've given them to help them make a sound buying decision.

Better yet, that means direct response advertising, compared to institutional advertising, asks for a response NOW. Thus, even one ad can bring in cash within days or weeks.

Be sure to include a response device, such as a coupon or special hotline phone number.

Something so that you can measure your responses.

One final and important point: Because most businesses focus on institutional advertising, direct response can yet again help to positively differentiate your business from your competitors.

Have you heard of the saying, 'what you can measure you can manage'?

By its very nature, direct response advertising brings in a response that can be measured so you can systematically test different ads, compare one against the other, and analytically determine which one works best.

SECTION 1: ADVERTISING & LETTER WRITING TO HELP YOU WIN NEW CUSTOMERS

Because these types of ad produce something you can track, analyse, and count, you can measure the profitability and performance of virtually every direct response ad.

Institutional advertising, on the other hand, produces no immediate measurable results, and so you're left wondering if you received value for your investment in that ad.

A better return on your investment can be achieved with direct response advertising.

Advertising can be a very costly way to acquire new customers. You pay for your ad to appear in a magazine or newspaper (or for your direct mail campaign), and only a small fraction of the consumers actually respond. Perhaps an even smaller percentage actually buys.

In principle, if an ad costs $500 and you get 50 responses, that means each response cost you $10. Unfortunately, you often only get 10 or perhaps even 5 responses, increasing your cost per response to $50 or $100. And if only 2 actually buy from you, each sale cost you $250! And you'd probably consider that expensive.

Given that, most businesses, large and small, just can't afford to do 'arty' institutional ads that get no sales. You need ads that are going to give you the greatest return on your investment in the space you just purchased to display that ad. Direct response ads are the way to go.

In almost every case, direct response advertising gives you infinitely more value, dollar for dollar, than institutional advertising. If you are running institutional ads, change them to direct response.

Give your prospects information that's important to them and adds value, instead of focusing inward!

By merely switching from institutional to direct response advertising, you can improve your productivity many times over. And leverage that investment in your advertising.

To improve your advertising and letter writing to win more new customers, target marketing rather than the 'shotgun' approach is important. That is, identifying your ideal customer or your 'customer profile/persona/avatar' can make your marketing more efficient and more results-driven.

Here you'll focus on targeting your marketing better to reach the potential customers you're after. You'll discover the value of aiming for a specific group of more responsive people – the right type of people for your product or service – instead of mass marketing, hoping against hope to hit the right targets.

Advertorials and direct response advertising rather than traditional advertising will also win more customers for you. Here's what's important in this area: writing headlines that really grab your readers, creating offers to entice people to you and win new business, guarantees, understanding the concept of 'WIIFM?" response devices, a call to action, and much more.

Check out the FREE 'Headline Analyser' tool from CoSchedule which will show you the quality strength of your title headline. https://coschedule.com/headline-analyzer

It is vital that all your advertising and marketing material talk about the benefits customers will receive rather than just the

SECTION 1: ADVERTISING & LETTER WRITING TO HELP YOU WIN NEW CUSTOMERS

features of your products or services or your business. For example, people don't want the drill they're purchasing at the hardware store – they want the hole it can make for them! So be sure and stick to explaining the benefits of your products and services. That way, people will be able to identify the value in it.

You see, it's important to educate to motivate customers to buy. If they don't fully understand what's in it for them, what benefits they can expect to gain and why one thing is better than another, they'll fail to make the right decision.

Using testimonials, graphics, layout technique, specific fonts, and lettering will keep people reading and will help educate them about your business.

Specific techniques should be applied to phone directory advertising. This is a different medium, and it requires some special attention to generate the best results possible.

Using a phone-mail-phone strategy – where you call to identify the right person to send a direct mail campaign to, send the campaign including key elements just mentioned, and then follow up by phone again – will always generate a greater response than a cold mailing.

Testing and measuring your advertising and direct mail techniques is mandatory to continually increase the response to your marketing. It could also save you thousands in lost dollars in mediums that just don't work. Without monitoring and measuring, you won't know if you're winning or losing on your marketing investment. In fact, it really will be more like a gamble.

Section 2

UCD's – are they still relevant?

People buy differences they perceive between one business and the next, between your business, for example, and your competitors.

Seth Godin, in his best-selling book *The Purple Cow*, says that the key to success in business is to find a way to stand out – to be the purple cow in a field of monochrome Holsteins. Create ways to make your business remarkable so that it stands out in its own right!

UCD's or Unique Core Differentiators clearly show the differences to your potential customers.

In fact, they help potential customers understand the added value, expertise, or service you might offer in a succinct, saleable way.

There are 3 kinds of UCDs.

The first is an actual UCD, something is genuinely unique about the way you do business.

The second is perceived, that is, people perceive your business or products or services to be different than your competitors, even if they actually are not that different!

SECTION 2: UCD'S – ARE THEY STILL RELEVANT?

And the third is a created UCD. Here, you create something different about your business – the way you serve people, the processes within your business, or how you actually serve customers.

I was privileged to see Simon Sinek – the world renowned expert on using a higher purpose to make your business stand out apart from the competition – live in Melbourne in March 2017.

In today's modern world, UCD's are giving way to 'purpose' driven businesses, businesses that matter or those that, according to Simon Sinek, can be differentiated because of 'clarity of why they do what they do'.

They also clearly have this front and centre of everything they do.

He goes further to say that "people do not buy what you do; they buy WHY you do what you do. People do not buy what you do; they buy what you BELIEVE in".

Have a look at why social enterprise 'thankyou' exists – "We believe we can end global poverty in this lifetime, together. That's why we give 100% of the profits from our awesome products to helping people in need. Almost a billion people live in extreme poverty, while six billion people don't. We reckon the six billion of us could work together to put an end to global poverty, for good."

So when you are looking to purchase a bottle of water to satisfy your thirst and you're faced in the supermarket with a choice of purchasing their generic brand or a 'thank you' bottle of water – if you're socially conscious and want to make a difference, you would automatically select the 'thankyou' bottle of water because you buy what they BELIEVE in!

When you know your 'why' your 'what' has more IMPACT – when you know how to clearly articulate your 'why', 'what' you do and 'how' you do it become profoundly more attractive and compelling!

At Ceebeks Business Solutions for GOOD, our 'why' (which we have given permission to feature in Adam Houlahan's best-selling book – The LinkedIn Playbook) is:

We get up every morning to positively impact young families in business to help them make their businesses really work so that together we can make an even greater impact. The rewards that brings allow our team, the 'fantastic four', to make small but powerful contributions to our local community, our country and in the lives of those less fortunate around the world.

Every interaction in our office with each other and the outside world has this message at its core.

You can easily over-complicate the process of coming up with your reason for being, for example: a WHY coach I read online, believes there are 9 and only 9 why's:

1. To contribute to a greater cause, make a difference, add value or have an impact
2. To create relationships based upon trust
3. To make sense out of things
4. To find a better way and share it
5. To do things the right way

SECTION 2: UCD'S – ARE THEY STILL RELEVANT?

6. To think differently & challenge the status quo
7. To seek mastery
8. To create clarity
9. To simplify

Or as Paul Dunn suggests, use your iPhone to record your response to "I get up every morning to…" which can be illustrated as follows:

To _____ so that _____
   (contribution)   (impact/effect you want to have on the world)

What do you think, all 9 or would just a simple statement help you find yours?

> **Chasers Tip** Check out Simon Sineks' TEDx talk on Youtube: *How Great Leaders Inspire Action*

Section 3

Sales systems & techniques

Selling is not the mystery everybody thinks it is. Put simply, people buy from people they trust. It's important to think of selling this way:

If a person inquires about something you do, they're asking for help in solving a problem or a need they might have. If you fail to do everything possible to give customers enough reasons to buy from you, you've done them a DISSERVICE.

This is particularly true if you know very well that you do offer a good quality product or service and that you may well be better at what you do than your competitors.

Regardless, they still have to go out there and find someone to help them solve this problem or a need. They still have to spend time and money looking for that person – who, at the end of the day, may not offer the value you do. So letting someone leave your business, someone who's already said they need help simply by being there, is a shame. And an expensive one!

SECTION 3: SALES SYSTEMS & TECHNIQUES

Creating ways of selling, such as a sales system and selling tools and techniques for your business, will build that trust and the sales themselves. Better yet, your customers will walk away happy, having just found the solution they were looking for.

A sales system could make & save you thousands of dollars.

If you're good at selling or if you have a team member who is good at selling, when you document what it is you or they do you've created a sales system.

Now before you think, 'That's too simple,' think again!

Really it *is* simple. (Ever noticed how all the great ideas usually are?)

Let's look into this further.

Good salespeople often go into what's called 'unconscious competence.' That is, they no longer remember why they specifically do or say certain things to potential customers, they just know ways and means to get a positive response.

Unconscious competence is a bit like driving a car. When you first learned to drive, you were fully aware of all of the rules in the exam you had to take before you even started the car. You had to know them to pass and get your licence.

Things like putting the keys in the ignition, moving the seat to a comfortable position, putting on your seatbelt, checking your rear view mirror, checking your side mirrors, starting the car in park, checking oncoming traffic, releasing the emergency brake, indicating your exit from the parked position, and so on.

Now as a competent driver you're no longer aware you're completing those steps.

You just do them automatically.

By rote or *'off by heart'*.

In fact as a competent driver it is actually difficult to identify all of those rules now.

That's unconscious competence.

It's the same for great salespeople. They become so competent that they forget the steps they're taking and just focus on the task at hand.

Because of this, the best way to create a sales system is to have yourself or your salesperson record 1 or 2 weeks of sales meetings and have those tapes transcribed.

Or have another person go to sales appointments with you or follow you through your premises when you're talking with customers, all the while taking notes. And break it down from there.

Those notes should cover what you said, when you said it, how the customer responded, how you handled any objections, any particular benefits you mentioned, and so on. Afterward that person can ask you why you did this or that at certain points. This will help gain an understanding of why you do what you do, when you do it in the sales process, and why that works.

Sometimes it's better if the person taking notes actually doesn't know that much about your business. They tend to ask more questions about certain aspects of the process than someone else who might also have unconscious competence!

From here you document all the information: how to get things started with a potential customer, greetings, questions, benefits to explain, the detailed questions to ask for the sale, how to handle objections, right through to how to complete any required paperwork for the sale. Ideally you might create a form for your team members to use as a thought jogger.

By doing this, you will create your sales system.

From there, you can set about training everybody to complete sales in this same way and sales *will* increase for *every* sales-related team member.

Think about the financial effect that could have on your business. If you could double the sales made by every team member, for example, just imagine what that would add to your business.

Interestingly, too, most business owners think they need to get more leads. The truth is, the business as a whole needs to convert more of the leads you do get. A sales system can help you do just that.

In a typical business, one or two team members generate much higher sales than the rest of the team. When this happens over and over again, this can be slightly demoralising for other team members. Some will never be certain of what they're doing wrong or what those very successful team members are doing so differently.

A sales system, with people fully trained to use the techniques in that system, gives everybody the chance to do just as well.

To see how an example of a sales system refer to Appendix 3.

When implemented properly and with every team member 'on-board' with the new system, sales will greatly be improved as a transformation comes over your business.

Suddenly everybody is trained in what works and has the ability to improve. People become happier in their work, their stats improve, and it's exciting to get better results. Often they feel they're doing a better job, and their confidence and morale increases. Plus your resources are being used more efficiently rather than continuing with what doesn't work!

Better yet, potential customers will be better served.

Further if you as the owner are the best salesperson or 'rain-making' as it is also sometimes called, this is almost the only way you can replace yourself AND guarantee that sales will continue to do well while you focus on other areas in your business.

The other advantage of a sales system is that you can never become beholden to one particular salesperson. Like a business in the fruit and vegetable supply industry turning over $20 million did.

This business owner became trapped in a losing situation. His key salesperson, someone who was responsible for a significant percentage of tomato sales, simply kept demanding more and more money each year. So much so that his salary reached $250,000 and he still wanted more. The business owner was in a no-win situation. If he fired the salesperson, sales would drop dramatically. However, he just couldn't afford to keep on forking out thousands on demand.

A sales system means that the salesperson is only as good as that system and so is replaceable.

So what's a practical way to uncover customer preferences and deal with this issue?

SECTION 3: SALES SYSTEMS & TECHNIQUES

Consider using the '6 Questions Test'

The '6 questions test' is one such tool that is designed to give you insight about the customers preferences when looking to make a decision to buy that could help you increase sales significantly.

This will be particularly true if you're working in a highly competitive market, where some competitors might be slashing prices only because they can! That is, they simply don't have the costs you carry because your business offers greater professionalism or experience and so on.

This tool will help educate your customers to what to look for *before* they commit to purchasing. And they will begin to understand why it's important to choose you. It further differentiates you from your competitors.

Remember: Customers buy the differences they perceive about your business.

Given that, it is critical that customers understand the differences between you and your competitors. Specifically, why what you offer is better than your competitors.

In fact, it is pivotal to tell every potential customer, in a benefit-oriented way, what your business does AND explain the way your business does it, so customers can spot those differences more easily.

The complete range of the products, services, expertise, and experience available through your business should be documented in a way that reminds current customers of the value of your service and lets any potential customers know why your business is better.

To see a practical example of the 6 Questions test check out Appendix 4.

Mapping out sales forecasts is also crucial to increasing sales. You see, it's much easier to get to where you're going – if you know where that is! Sales forecasts help you find that direction and give you a solid path to follow!

Some other issues to consider are cross-selling, upselling, and packaging products or services together.

When the young salesperson at McDonalds asks, "Would you like some french fries with that?" – that's a cross-selling system in action.

What could cross-selling do for your business?

You see, cross-selling – selling other items from 'across' your range at the same time as the customers make their initial purchase – is a vital concept. It's a selling style that contributes greatly to the third way to grow your business, that is, to increase your average sale.

Most business owners focus their marketing energy on winning customers. Getting customers to come back more often is vital to the long-term health and profitability of your business.

By understanding this issue, you could add more value to your customers and increase your profitability.

Revisit Chapter 3 – Increase the Average Sale of each Sale, you see, often people don't know or don't think about other items or services that might add to the first product or service they intend to purchase. You need to suggest some ideas. Ideas that would increase the average sale for your business.

Conversion rates – the difference between the number of inquiries you receive and the number of sales you make – are like taking the sales pulse of your business.

Not tracking could be affecting your financial position, team morale, and more.

When you have these conversion rates, you can then work to improve them, increasing sales to boot!

Most businesses owners look to increase their businesses by finding new leads. Most focus on generating more and more inquiries.

Amazingly though, most wouldn't have a clue how many of their current inquiries actually become sales – they simply don't know whether they're winning or losing!

That is, they fail to track their conversion rates.

Your conversion rate is the difference between the number of inquiries received and the number of sales made.

This can then be calculated as a percentage.

You simply must do this – track your conversion rates – to grow your business.

For most businesses, focusing on generating MORE inquiries will get you nowhere. Instead you need to be doing MORE with the ones you've got!

You see, sales opportunities are staring you in the face. As you probably know right now, there's no doubt you're losing sales opportunities every day. The question really is... how many? And what could happen to your business and your profits if you could win more?

To find out, you need to develop a system for tracking 'conversion rates' and the sales generated for your business.

To get that process started, answer this question:

'Of the inquiries you receive, what percentage do you think turn into sales?'

Make a mental note or write your answer here: _____%

Interestingly, when most business owners or team members are asked, the majority will say:

"Oh about 75%. Yeah, I think 70, 75%."

Some would be a little more conservative and suggest "about 50 or 60%."

When then asked:

Is that fact? Do you specifically track that somehow, or is it a guesstimate?'

Most business owners will agree it's only a guesstimate. If this is true for you, your business could be facing a MONUMENTAL opportunity. An opportunity you couldn't have asked for!

And that's because when most business owners actually track their conversion rates, most find it's often actually as low as 20% or 26%, to a maximum of about 32% or 35%.

It becomes obvious, then, that generating leads is in fact the least of your worries.

It's clear **CONVERTING** your existing leads into sales is the greatest opportunity for your business – NOT generating new leads!

Fact is, you're already generating plenty of leads. You have more than you can convert, so that must be your focus.

SECTION 3: SALES SYSTEMS & TECHNIQUES

This will improve your profitability, too. You see, it costs you perhaps thousands to make your phone ring or have people visit your premises. Every single one of those leads costs you money. Each one that you fail to convert increases the costs of winning those customers that you do. Converting more means you make more on each new customer you win, and your cost per sale decreases proportionately.

Better yet, this is a fantastic opportunity for the business.

It's easy to do (and some examples for you)

You'll remember, your conversion rate is the number of inquiries received compared to the number of sales made, as a percentage.

Conversion rates can be tracked in several ways.

Clearly you must track the *number* of incoming calls or inquiries and then the number of sales made from there. This could be done on a simple tally sheet or through other systems, such as keeping all proposals or quotes numbered and comparing that to the weekly or monthly sales figures.

These calls or inquiries could then be broken down further into the source of the call. So, in fact, you have a conversion rate tracking system and a marketing tracking system all in one simple process or form.

For example, your sources of business could include:

1. Advertising
2. Referral
3. Mail
4. Drive-by/walk-in

5. e-Book downloads
6. Host-style relationship
7. Flyer
8. Current client
9. Other...

Simply by asking:

"Oh and just before you go, could I ask how you heard about us?"
or
"And, [Inquirer's Name], how did you hear about us?"

You'll be able to measure not only your conversion rate but also the source of the inquiry.

In fact, you could create a table that looks something like the next one. And use this as a tally sheet every day to track the number of inquiries versus the number of sales. For example, the slashes in the columns represent the number of inquiries from the source. The check marks and x's represent the total sales made or lost from those inquiries.

Day	Advert	Referral	Mail	Walk-in	eBook	Host	Flyer	Current Customer	Other	Sold	Follow up
Mon	\\		\\\				\	\\	\	✓✓✓ xxx	\\
Tue											
Wed											
Thu											
Fri											
Sat											
Sun											

SECTION 3: SALES SYSTEMS & TECHNIQUES

This tally sheet could be kept by each person or it could be left beside the cash register. Or you could use a more detailed system, such as numbering quotes and proposals and comparing that to sales numbers. Regardless, it should be easy to track and tracked weekly or monthly, depending on your type of business.

Ideally, you'll develop this system to then track, very specifically, the conversion rates of each team member for 'potential client inquiries.' To do that, each team member could have a separate sheet or initial any inquiries or sales they record. You'd then collate them at the end of every week, for example.

To increase these conversion rates and have your team feel very comfortable with the selling process, either over the phone or face-to-face, you'll need to develop some scripts, basic points, checklists, and responses to handle those inquiries and potential sales in the best possible way – every time.

Follow-up systems are critical here, too. 80% of sales are made after the 5th contact. That makes it well worth your while to find out more about this area.

Body language can also be a tool or work against you in a sales situation. This should also be reviewed. Are you and/or your team showing a genuine interest in helping solve a potential customer's problem or are they just an inconvenience? Your body language will show and reflect that to the customer.

At a recent small business event we held in my hometown of Warrnambool with Paul Dunn – Unleashing the HUGE Power of Small to Build an Amazing Business in these Amazing Times, Paul suggested that the simple rephrasing of words can make a huge difference to the way in which a proposal is presented to a potential customer.

He went further to say that avoiding the word 'quote' could also increase your sales. Simply put, most people will associate the word 'quote' with price. And because it's not a good idea generally to have your potential customers focused on price, the word has to go!

Something out of the 'Useful box' (see further on in this section at Chapter 11), different ideas, terrific tools to capture passing trade such as good, clear legible signage that is noticeable and readable, and using merchandising techniques can also improve sales.

'Professional selling' – creating the opportunity and the rapport, understanding the prospective customer's real needs by asking detailed questions, selling on 'purpose,' talking in the customer's language, gathering feedback at every step, making it easy for your customers to buy from you, empathising with their concerns and reassuring the customer – are all crucial steps in the sales process.

Section 4

The phone

Despite undergoing such a dramatic change over the past 15 years or so, the humble phone is still today one of the most wasted resources in business!

Ever had the experience of someone so gruff, rude or unpleasant on the end of the phone when you have called or been left hanging on the seemingly unending ring tone of your call waiting for someone to pick up and answer your call?

Most people treat callers with disdain: 'How dare you interrupt my busy day!'

And most just don't know how to convert an inquiry over the phone to a sale. Worse yet, many just don't have a clue about general phone manners.

Some are afraid to use to the phone to follow up with potential customers or to generate new leads, not being sure what to say and so on. These issues MUST be addressed if you're going to truly grow your business and leverage your marketing dollars.

The development of minimum performance standards over the phone and the use of phone scripts to handle both incoming and outgoing phone calls may alleviate some of that anxiety, increase conversions, and increase sales.

Most business owners are looking to improve their advertising or their direct mail, for example, so they can generate more inquiries. Unfortunately, because of poor phone techniques and a lack of team training, most businesses are not doing enough with the leads they're already getting – so why go out and spend a fortune and generate more only to burn them on the other end of the phone line?

On the other hand, simply improving phone handling and over-the-phone techniques is a pivotal area for increasing sales and profitability.

If you will, the phone can be likened to the 'front line' of battle.

It literally is the front line between you and your customers. It's often the first place you and your potential customers meet. It's often the very first contact between your potential customer and your team members. So on the business battlefield, it's just as important as a real front line.

The way a customer is dealt with from the moment that phone is answered can fundamentally make the difference for the sale.

Further, it's also the most common means a customer uses to stay in touch with you.

Given that, then, it is imperative that the phone is handled with consummate skill.

Before you think, 'Well, my junior staff member just hasn't got the experience to have 'consummate' skill,' rest easy.

SECTION 4: THE PHONE

There is a solution – a system.

A system so that every customer call is handled in the same professional, courteous way each and every time. A system that sets the minimum standard required and agreed to by team members – performance standards.

The system and standards create 'sameness,' a consistency, for your team and your customers.

You'll agree: Creating an agreed way of dealing with people over the phone is critical, and using standard systemised way for handling all calls consistently is a great way to get a call started.

However, you also need to address other issues such as furthering a brilliant image with callers and setting more standards to address transferring calls, taking messages and so on – standards that really would set you apart.

Most importantly, creating sales from apparently casual calls and effectively dealing with the 'how much is it?' phone call is vital to generate a better return on your marketing dollar and increase sales. A certain finesse is needed over the phone to create meetings with people that matter. Handling complaints successfully is important, too.

Check out Appendix 7 Performance Standards for your Phone for ideas and techniques to use to dramatically differentiate your business, leave a lasting impression and convert more inquiries into customers.

Section 5

Other promotions

Tools like promotions schedules can help you win new customers. One of the keys to marketing is being constant and consistent – tech tools like Facebook, Instagram, Pinterest allow you more than ever to build a brand presence and promote to a wider audience at a fraction of the cost. Consider using automated promotion schedules with apps like Zoho, Buffer, Hootsuite, Infusionsoft and my favourite, Hubspot, help you maintain activity and so maintain sales to new customers.

Creating special events, holding value-added seminars and competitions could all assist in winning new customers. The recent small business event we held in my hometown of Warrnambool with Paul Dunn – Unleashing the HUGE Power of Small to Build an Amazing Business in these Amazing Times, gave us access to several new prospects and two new customers.

Something as simple as a special Facebook Community for your ideal customers to be part of where valuable tips, ideas and

SECTION 5: OTHER PROMOTIONS

information can be shared gives them a reassured sense of belonging to a tribe with the same ideals.

We have created a Facebook Community – Chasing the Dream – for those customers and prospects of ours. This is a place where it is more important to help someone else than to promote yourself. It is a place where help by collaboration becomes natural.

This group is where we give advice and support to individuals, couples and families about improving their businesses and their financial lifestyle, after all we might just be 'living the dream' if we can tweak a couple of really important areas in the 'money-side' of our lives.

This group is run by me, but it is not about me or even for me. It is for everyone who is passionate about helping others and who wants to improve their business, their financial wellbeing, and ultimately their lifestyle.

The purpose of the Facebook Community – Chasing the Dream is as follows:

> "This is YOUR community as long as you add value.
> This group is a place to get answers about issues such as:
> How to start a business and get off the ground.
> How to make a plan for your lifestyle
> How to create a better cash flow for your business
> How to have more time by doing things better by challenging why it is being done that way
> How to use technology to run a smarter business

How to promote your business using Social media, podcasts, Blogs, & eBooks

How to get more customers

Share stories about your business journey, product launch or success tips.

> **Chasers Tip** When you post anything you are doing that works really well for you or post something that you want to know more about, please do so in the appropriate thread just make sure you ADD Value (don't just drop a link – this is basic marketing and human interaction).

A few other guidelines:

- Support other people regularly (we promise it will help you more than spamming a link)
- Lead with your heart and be honest (ask the hard questions you want to know about money and financial matters)
- Promote other people's stuff, e.g. their ideas, business practices or charitable works because you want to help (not make money)
- Be a good person (don't 'bag' anyone else!)
- Ask yourself (Who can this help?) each time you post

SECTION 5: OTHER PROMOTIONS

- This is intended to be a considerate, passionate, and helpful group to collaboratively grow each other's business or improve our financial health, and in turn, impact our collective lifestyles."

Get the idea of how a special Facebook Community for your ideal customers and those potential ones you want to attract?

Improving direct mail, catalogues, trade show exhibits and strategies... TV and radio... and generating more free publicity through public relations – all these can also increase people's positive exposure to your business.

Networking, partnering with other like-minded businesses, having other businesses sell for you, winning leads from competitors, or tapping into buying lists from other companies can give you access to new customers you may not have otherwise reached.

Harnessing the power of 'word of mouth' by creating a referral system could, in fact, double your business for very little investment. You see, almost every business owner, perhaps yourself, too, feels that 'word of mouth' – customers talking about you to others – is a huge source of business. And yet, most do not have a system in place to capture these referrals regularly. Most simply leave the customers to their own devices and hope for the best.

Now imagine what would happen if every single customer you had was invited to refer at least one other possible customer to you?

You could double your customer base!

At the very worst, you'd increase the number of people referred to your business every day!

Better yet, people who've been referred to you are, in fact, four times more likely to buy from you. You see, they already trust you because they trust the person who referred you!

Another very powerful tool here is establishing host-style arrangements, where you and a noncompeting business with the same type of customers complete on going, joint promotions to each other's customer bases.

This means that you could access twice your customer base of your ideal type of customers, not just anyone mind you, in a blink of the eye.

And because these arrangements usually mean that the business is endorsing you to a customer, that customer is again four times more likely to buy from you.

Section 6

Junk Mail – may not be junk after all!

Some businesses pay thousands of dollars to marketing and advertising gurus to develop and research ways and ideas to get their customers to buy from them.

Those ways and ideas often make their way to your business in the form of 'junk' mail.

What do you do with this junk mail?

Do you throw it away without too much thought?

Each time you do this, you could be throwing away valuable ideas (that someone else has spent thousands of dollars getting researched, designed and produced) and in the process costing yourself time and money!

That's where the wonderfully simple to execute "Useful Box" strategy comes into play. The next time you embark on the wastebasket shuffle, rather than thinking junk mail, change the way you look at this sometimes valuable resource.

Instead, view the volumes of material that enter your life as a source of awesome ideas, business.

> **Chasers Tip** A Useful Box is a place where you store ideas (usually generated from advertisements or junk mail) that might be of some use to you when you're developing new marketing ideas. It is also a special folder stored on your PC or in the cloud in Box for easy retrieval and access for storing the electronic junk mail ideas you receive every day!

Here are three simple steps that I have used over the past 27 years when looking at marketing ideas from junk mail:

Step 1: Keep it simple.
Get yourself a decent sized box and store it in a highly visible place in your business.

You know the saying out of sight, out of mind? It's absolutely the case with this strategy.

Make sure your Useful Box is visible by all members of the team. This will ensure it is used more frequently than if it is stashed neatly in a cupboard and forgotten!

You'll probably find it too difficult to construct a filing system that will accommodate the variety of examples you'll accumulate.

You'll either waste time figuring out where to file, or you'll waste time trying to figure out where it's been filed!

We've found that the most effective way is simply to throw it all into a box and rummage through it when you need an idea. Often you'll stumble across something else you can use in the process that you forgot you'd collected!

Step 2: Assess everything you're sorting before it lands in the box, and educate your team to do the same.

Does it have Useful Box potential? Once you're aware of the value of this sort of material, we guarantee you'll start to view everything through a different set of eyes. For example, have you ever stayed in a hotel that had a good customer feedback questionnaire in the room?

Or have you ever been to a restaurant that had an unusual competition running?

Have you ever been given a business card that really jumped out at you? (Ask Paul Dunn to see his business card – it really leaves an impression and stands out clearly from all others!)

Encourage your team to be constantly on the lookout for these powerful tools. Introduce a Useful Box Contributions section into your team meetings. This lets everyone know what material is being added each week and helps the team to become involved.

You'll be surprised at how quickly you'll accumulate an excellent range of examples.

Step 3: Use it!
Obvious?

Yes.

And the most critical step. The only way you'll benefit from creating this Useful Box is to make good use of its contents. You'll save valuable time and avoid the challenge of needing to become an instant marketing expert overnight by drawing on the experience of others.

Let's use your own business as an example. You've decided to introduce a structured referral system and you (or one of your team) remember an excellent referral idea discovered last month at the local optometrist.

You dig through the Useful Box, find the piece in question, and half your work is done for you.

The other benefit of having an active Useful Box strategy is that you and your team will often come up with more creative suggestions simply as a result of being exposed to so many different ideas and examples.

What Should You Look For?

Basically, anything that catches your eye is Useful Box material.

If it grabs your attention, it's working. Chances are it will grab the attention of your customers too.

SECTION 6: JUNK MAIL – MAY NOT BE JUNK AFTER ALL!

Brochures, letters, gift certificates, advertisements, magazine inserts, frequent shopper cards, great letters – these are just a few of the formats this material will present itself to you in.

The key content items to be on the lookout for are:

- *Offers designed to generate a rapid response or to "act now"*
- *Differentiation/unique core differentiator strategies*
- *Customer retention strategies*
- *Loyalty programs/frequent shopper campaigns*
- *Referral strategies*
- *The second dimension (see article on page 2)*
- *Guarantees*
- *Gift vouchers (e.g., $X off your purchase)*
- *Demographic-targeted marketing campaigns*
- *Attention-grabbers/very creative pieces*

Creating a Useful Box is a simple strategy, but one that can save you a lot of time and creative energy.

Take a little time to implement the 3-step plan outlined above.

You'll soon see the fruits of that investment repaid many times over.

As the saying goes – 'one man's trash is another man's treasure' – use it to your advantage!

Section 7

Become a key person of influence

Every industry has a 'guru' – you know, the go to person whose name comes up in conversations relating to it. They seem to attract customers, opportunity and earn more money.

They are known as 'key persons of influence'.

These people quite often have followed a proven system outlined by Daniel Priestly, in his best-selling book – *Key Persons of Influence* by following these 5 principles:

1. Create a pitch, this is similar to the elevator pitch. Basically, figure out what you do and why you do it and whenever anyone asks what you do, you can articulate to them what it is very clearly and with confidence and poise.
2. Write a book, build up your credibility base with these types of assets.
3. Create something to sell. Basically turn your book into a DVD, or download.

SECTION 7: BECOME A KEY PERSON OF INFLUENCE

4. Be on the front page of Google search results.
5. Find other people who offer complementary products or services and team up with them. Bring your audience for your partner to sell to and sell to his audience.

This strategy for winning new customers requires time and patience to cultivate and nurture and works extremely well for service-based industries.

By developing into a key person of influence in your market, you will become the expert in that area, the name that's dropped whenever that topic comes up and you will have customers who need your service – qualified leads – contacting you for help.

You establish more credibility, trust and an air of knowledge and draw customers to you.

Sometimes turning your services into 'products' can improve the processes within your business dramatically. In fact, this strategy could put you head and shoulders above your competition.

Service businesses in particular need to start thinking about their services as products and setting up processes in their businesses to do so. That way, they'll get clear on the hard costs of delivering that 'product' and so on. They begin to treat their business operations like a production-based business. By doing so, profits could increase significantly.

Daniel Priestly is a huge advocate for packaging up services into products and views them as part of the product ecosystem that help educate, inspire and relate to more people. They not only differentiate you as a business but also can develop into another source of revenue.

Understanding your real purpose of being in business and establishing the 'why' of your business can help you build better processes to meet that purpose and increase sales with customers. It can also give your team members clearer direction. Establishing yourself as a key person of influence can do this.

Final thoughts

There has never been a time like the one we are currently living in! The shrinking of the global economy, through the access and the use of remarkable technologies, allows us to talk and see people around the world in real time and to do business with them. We can design digital products or services that can be viewed anywhere, anytime. We can do more with less much more quickly and efficiently and really challenge traditional ways of doing things and disrupt the status quo.

Opportunity is really now here – in fact it's everywhere!

However, in the wise words of Seth Godin, 'the challenge is not to be successful; the challenge is to matter'.

When designing your new business or re-inventing an existing one for these amazing times hopefully you will choose to matter more!

If you set aside time to work **ON** your business and not **IN** it, and work on articulating 'why' you are in business, develop your true purpose and look to create a business than serves above selling; you are well on your way to building an amazing meaningful business, one that matters to you, your customers and the world.

Your business, no matter how big it is, could even make a global impact!

That's right.

By doing what you do every day in your business, you could help transform a life, impact a village and change the world.

How?

By joining B1G1 – Business for Good, a social enterprise and non-profit organisation with a mission to create a world full of giving.

Unlike conventional giving models, B1G1 helps small – and medium-sized businesses achieve more social impact by embedding giving activities into everyday business operations and creating unique giving stories. Every business transaction (and as a result, the business' day-to-day activity) can impact lives for as little as just one cent.

In fact at the time of writing B1G1 members have made more than 192,000,000 impacts globally in many of these areas.

And the best part is that businesses of every size, particularly small businesses can make huge contributions through the power of small, regular giving.

B1G1 has closely aligned its projects with the 17 Sustainable Development Goals of the United Nations to help build a better world. They are a powerful set of idealistic goals but with the help of organisations like, B1G1, are rapidly becoming achievable.

SECTION 7: BECOME A KEY PERSON OF INFLUENCE

As an added bonus, partnering with B1G1 allows you to develop, identify and clarify your purpose, your 'WHY' for doing what you do too! Furthermore, you can access mentors and participate in 'Mastermind' online meet ups within your global B1G1 family to really play a 'bigger game'.

So, you can grow your business in these amazing times when you combine all of this groundwork and focus your efforts on the four main ways to grow your business:

1. Increase the number of customers (*of the type you want*);
2. Increase the number of times customers come back;
3. Increase your average value of each sale; and
4. Improve the effectiveness of each process in your business you should see the rewards and successes for your efforts.

And if some of your rewards and successes can be shared through creating more impacts in this world on the lives of those less fortunate than ourselves, then together we can create a world that is full of giving and sharing – a much better place for our next generation.

There has never been a time to matter more!

> "Let's you and I explore this next great frontier where the boundaries between work and higher purpose are merging into one; where doing good really is good for business"
> — Sir Richard Branson.

Go, chase your dream, make an impact and matter in these amazing times we live in!

Part Three

Appendix 1

Using 3 Ways to Dramatically Grow Your Business

Complete the figures below for your business and calculate the results:

_____ x _____ x $_____ = $_____

Now calculate for yourself what happens when EACH area is increased by 10% at the same time, like in the example in Chapter 1.

1,100 x 1.1 x $110 = $_____ Turnover!

That's right – increasing each area at the same time has a multiplier effect of increasing turnover NOT by 10% like you could assume, but by a staggering 33.1%!

An additional income of not 10% to $110,000 but 33.1% to $133,100! An increase of $33,100 in turnover for doing nothing else except improving EACH area at once rather than concentrating on just one area at a time.

This multiplier effect is caused by the combination, the momentum, of all 3 areas working together. Each impacts the other. So once more, rather than a 10% growth factor, the momentum created by working on EACH one of these first key areas brings about a growth of 33.1%!

Try this calculation on your own business now.

_____ x _____ x $_____ = $_____ Turnover!

The increase should surprise, impress, and last but not least have you jumping out of your seat with excitement.

Appendix 2

Your Own Ideal Customer Persona Traits Template

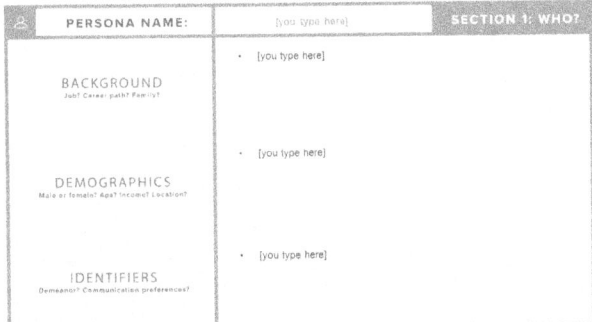

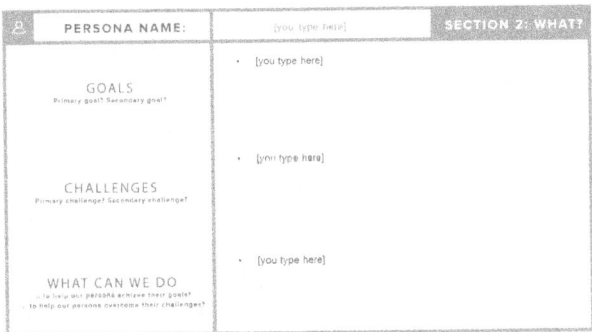

CHASING THE DREAM!

PERSONA NAME:	[you type here]	SECTION 3: WHY?
REAL QUOTES
About goals, challenges, etc.	• [you type here]	
COMMON OBJECTIONS
Why wouldn't they buy your product/service?	• [you type here]	

PERSONA NAME:	[you type here]	SECTION 4: HOW?
MARKETING MESSAGING
How should you describe your solution to your persona?	• [you type here]	
ELEVATOR PITCH
Sell your persona on your solution.	• [you type here]	

Appendix 3

A Sales System Example

You've probably been in a retail pharmacy environment, a Chemist Warehouse type size store, one where you might find as many as 6 to 8 retail assistants serving customers behind the counter and on the retail floor. So let's review a case from this kind of business.

As mentioned earlier, in these environments as in most businesses, 1 or 2 assistants will always sell up to *twice* as much as the others. That's double the sales from one retail assistant to another!

And it's not that they're particularly different or better than their counterparts. It's not because of any specific education, training, or age. It's just that they've found a way of dealing with people that works.

Works for the customers, for them, and for the business as a whole. It usually means they've found a better way of helping customers find what they need. Let's take a closer look through the contrasting scenarios below.

Scenario 1

A customer walks into a Chemist Warehouse and asks the sales assistant where she can find Band-Aids. This assistant, one who doesn't sell huge amounts by the way, physically points to the area where that item is found. As she points, she might say something like this:

'Turn left at the nappies, right at the nail polish, and just after the beauty products you'll find the Band-Aids.'

Knowing that pharmacies can literally have thousands of items in stock, this can seem quite rude and a little daunting for customers, particularly if they're in a hurry or have the kids in tow! Nevertheless, they go off in the direction they were 'pointed' to look for the Band-Aids.

Scenario 2

A customer walks into a smaller boutique pharmacy and asks the sales assistant where she can find Band-Aids. This assistant, one who sells twice as much, might smile and say something like this:

'Thank you for dropping in. If you'd like to come with me, I'll take you right to them.'

'Oh really,' thinks the customer, 'yes, thank you, that would be great,' noting that no one else bothers to do that. On the way to the Band-Aids, the conversation might go as follows:

APPENDIX 3: A SALES SYSTEM EXAMPLE

'Specifically are you buying the Band-Aids for use at home or as part of a first aid kit or for a sporting team say?'

'Oh just for around the house. You know the kids are always tripping over things, getting little cuts and scrapes.'

The assistant might then comment: 'Yes, I understand. How many kids do you have?' The customer might reply 'Just the 3.' The assistant might then say:

'Keep you busy, I bet! This size box is probably the best for you. (As the assistant says that, he or she physically picks up the appropriate box and shows it to the customer.) *The other will run out too soon, and the bigger one is more suited to a soccer team!*'

By this stage the customer says, 'Yes, I'm sure you're right. I'll take that. Thanks.'

As the customer walks away, the assistant might say something like this:

'Before you go, there's nothing worse than getting home and realising you don't have everything you need for the kids. For example, do you have some antiseptic wash and cream to prevent infections on all those cuts and scrapes? Even the smallest ones can be a problem if not treated properly.'

'Actually, come to think of it, no I don't have any of that. You're right, I do need to get some.'

'Well let's head over to that section now and we'll find the right kind for you and your kids' needs...'

My partner, Angela, and I have experienced this first hand – scenario one from a huge Chemist Warehouse franchise and the second scenario from a smaller boutique pharmacy.

In comparing the two scenarios, one where the first assistant merely offers the smallest amount of help versus one where the second assistant actually *assists*, you can see the possibility for vastly increased sales – *and repeat business.*

This is particularly true when you imagine Scenario 2 every single time a customer walks into the store.

Imagine what a difference that would make!

This is specifically why the more helpful, friendly retail assistants, who welcome the customer, thank them, build rapport, genuinely offer help, and then make sure they have everything they need, sell up to double that of their counterparts.

Scenario 1 could be interpreted as 'perceived indifference' when compared to scenario 2.

Appendix 4

The '6 Questions Test'

The '6 Questions Test' is a great tool to assist in this process. This is a checklist, if you like, for your potential customers to work through. As they do that, they begin to understand the importance of some specific aspects, even technical aspects, of buying from your type of business.

By answering these questions, your customers will learn what it is they need to watch out for when making their buying decision – and, subtly, why yours is better.

They begin to understand why buying from you, despite a higher price, might be important. They begin to understand the value offered by your business. They begin to understand technical aspects of your business or your work that really will make a difference to them in the long run. They start to believe you offer them more protection and less risk of losing their money or making the wrong decision. They begin to feel more confident in buying from you and, conversely, less interested in buying from your competitors.

In short, it helps them make the right decision – to buy from you!

And that's simply because it's a very powerful positioning tool. It really will help them understand the differences between you and your competitors.

You see, statistics show that it is NOT so much price that makes a buying decision (in fact, only fifteen per cent of the market shops on price alone). Rather it's a *lack* of any other means of differentiating you over your competitors!

You see, when someone calls your business for the price and gets it without any other benefits or information, they then call the next person and the next and have the same experience. Finally, they call someone who gives them a different price. Sure enough – they decide to go with the lowest price. At this point, though, have they been given ANY other reason to buy? Do they have anything OTHER than price to differentiate you from your competitors?

No ...

... of course not.

But things might be different if they were to call someone who asked them some questions, explained a few things, gave them some material to read, clearly showed them the differences, the real benefits, of their products or services, (or business itself), and *only then* gave them a price. That person would be able to make a decision on something other than price, wouldn't they?

Of course they would.

In fact, they'd be far more likely to buy at that point. Your potential customers would finally be happy that someone had taken an interest in them and their needs instead of treating them with indifference.

APPENDIX 4: THE '6 QUESTIONS TEST'

(Statistics show that sixty-eight per cent of the people who call and then don't purchase do so because they feel you don't care enough about their needs – they perceive you couldn't care less whether they purchased from you. In other words, they perceive you're indifferent toward them).

This '6 Questions' test is just one tool to help you persuade customers to buy from you.

Better yet, you will have created a greater confidence in your business and your products and services *without* having to denigrate your competitors or actually say 'we're better.' From a customer's point of view, this is a far more appealing approach. And by using this tool, potential customers are simply better able to make that decision for themselves.

This '6 Questions' test can be created in such a way that you explain what is important for making sure potential customers receive the greatest benefits from your *type* of business, products, or services.

It could be titled:

'6 Questions you need to ask your [type of business] and how [your business name] answers them.'

'6 Questions you need to ask your [type of business] before you commit.'

This information can be packaged in various ways, such as an e-Book on your website, a brochure, a single page printed from your computer, or a flyer. As a tool, it can be used at various points in the sales process.

For example, let's say you get phone inquiries; however, you rarely actually sell your product or service over the phone. In this case, you'd be aiming to convert inquiries into meetings either at the potential customer's premises or yours, depending on your type of product or service. In this case, after you've set up a meeting, you could offer to send this information, as follows:

> 'Great, thank you for making that time to meet with me. Before we do that, I do have some interesting information that could be of help to you. It will also give you a better idea of what we do and how you'll benefit. [Potential Customer's Name], so that I can send that to you, what's the best address to use?'

By doing this at this point in the sales process, you're ensuring that potential customers will be warmer to you by the time you actually arrive for the meeting. Further, they'll be better informed if they speak to your competitors in the meantime. In fact, they'll be a little suspicious and so will tend to keep the appointment.

Some businesses could use this actual '6 Questions' test as an advertisement in itself. Others would use it as a sales tool to give customers before they visit the business or at the end of that first meeting, to keep them interested and prepare them for their second. Others might have it in poster format hanging on the walls of the premises. Others could use the checklist as an offer. For example:

> 'Call 1800-555555 now to receive your copy of 'The 12 Questions you Need to Ask Before You Renovate Your Home' report, valued at $22.95.'

APPENDIX 4: THE '6 QUESTIONS TEST'

Ideally, this information should be technical, or at the very least talk about detail. It should explain issues your customers, or a 'layperson' would otherwise not know. The example included later will give you a better understanding.

You see, when you use this tool to educate potential customers about issues they otherwise simply wouldn't know – the more detailed or technical it is –

(a) the better value it has; and
(b) the more believable it is.

It no longer feels like a piece of marketing hype.

It is actually valuable information and really could help someone new at dealing with your kind of business or at buying your product or service.

Plus, being detailed, the answers to these questions can clearly show the difference between you and a competitor.

Bear in mind, you don't have to limit yourself to just 6 technical questions and answers. Use as many as possible to make your potential customers question the services and products or standard of business they should be dealing with.

Make these e-Books, brochures or flyers available to all your prospects.

It does two things:

1. It nurtures your potential customers; and
2. gives your products and services a higher perceived value.

Better yet, by educating your customers, you'll come across as the leader in your market, the most professional. Potential customers will appreciate the information and feel you care about delivering a quality product or service.

By working through this example, you'll gain an understanding of just how powerful this '6 Questions' test can be as an educational tool. This example could be used by an events business, one that would organise special events, for instance. We'll call them 'Memorable Events'

6 Questions You Need to Ask Your Event Entertainment Crew and How Memorable Events Answers Them

Q1. Does the entertainment company take care of absolutely everything for you?

Memorable Events ✓ Others ?

You're a busy person, aren't you?
Because of that, the last thing you probably need is to have to take care of another thousand things!

Like finding an appropriate venue or making your existing venue 'event ready,' finding staff, training them, and having them fully prepared. From designing the audio and visual aspects of the event, co-ordinating entertainers, getting people to come,

APPENDIX 4: THE '6 QUESTIONS TEST'

arranging catering or sponsorship, generating some free publicity, making sure everything is in place, and much, much more.

That's why it's vital to make sure any event company you're talking with takes care of ALL the details for you.

Interestingly, at Memorable Events, we work through a thorough checklist (exclusive to Memorable Events) of 124 items to make sure absolutely everything is perfect and your event is a well-organised, huge success. Ask to see a copy of this checklist if you like. It really will give you an idea of just what lengths we go to to make your event goes off without a hitch.

Q2. Does the entertainment company work to make it a profitable event?

Memorable Events ✓ Others ?

For example, do they take care of the marketing for the event—designing and distributing your posters, flyers, and tickets? Oftentimes, inviting people to your event and having a great crowd show up is affected solely by your marketing. Whether you're holding the event as a fundraiser or a money-making venture, the numbers on the night directly affect your profits.

Unfortunately, most companies expect you to do your own marketing, preferring to focus on the logistics of your event.

It's really important, then, to be sure to check that any event entertainment company you're talking with takes care of your marketing for you. It's important, too, to make sure they're good at it! Be sure and ask about their track record in getting numbers to events and so on.

Of course, at Memorable Events, we feel that 'there's no party without punch' and consider marketing that critical aspect of organising your event.

Q3. Does the entertainment company have a 100% safety record?

Memorable Events ✓ | Others ?

In these days of litigation and commercial risk, the risk you carry in holding these sorts of events is high. That's why it's important your entertainment company has a good safety record, preferably one without incident, from events they've held in the past.

Of course, at Memorable Events, not a single incident has ever occurred.

Q4. Does the entertainment company have Public Liability Insurance?

Memorable Events ✓ | Others ?

This insurance is your protection, so it's vital to make absolutely sure public liability is in place. That way, you're totally protected should a mishap take place during the event. Memorable Events is covered to the value of $50 million, so you can rest assured you're covered.

Q5. Does the entertainment company have 'XYZ' and 'ABC' equipment?

Memorable Events ✓ | Others ?

This is important because XYZ equipment allows the entertainment crew to create a spectacular laser light and audio show that will make a really great impression. Not only that, ABC equipment means that the tone of the event can be, literally, changed with the flick

APPENDIX 4: THE '6 QUESTIONS TEST'

of a switch. With only 3 XYZ and 4 ABC in the entire country, this equipment can mean the difference between a mediocre event and a fantastic experience that people will talk about for months to come.

Q6. Does the entertainment company help you create a theme for your event?

Memorable Events ✓ Others ?

Every event needs to be 'themed'; that is, every event should have a theme of colours and styles that carries through from marketing to the lighting. Each event needs a title or a slogan to build it into something more than just your average party or event. This theming needs to match your organisation's image, the kind of people you want to attract, your own logo colours, and the style of entertainment being produced.

Further, themes like fancy dress or fun topics can be a great way to excite people about an event. It can also mean your event might get some free publicity before and after the event in the society pages or business sections of local papers.

With 25 years' experience and just over 3,426 events under our belt – ranging from the Grand Openings to Corporate Balls and Cocktail Parties to New Business Openings to School Dance Parties – the team at Awesome Events can help you create a theme that matches your needs (and your budget) perfectly.

So how could you use the '6 Questions' test or some version of it in your business to increase sales and your professionalism in the eyes of your potential customers?

Appendix 5

Positive cash flow and good debtor control

Fortunately, there are different ways to shorten your cash cycle. You can use your existing relationship with your customers to eliminate the time between cash flow cycles. By understanding who your customers are and when they are paid, for example, you can time your billing procedures to coincide with your customers' regular pay cycle. You can also entice customer to pay faster by offering them some type of incentive to pay sooner rather than later. You can also get your bills out to your customers sooner to help speed up the pay process.

Many people generally play roles in the billing and invoicing process. It is possible in many cases to increase the overall speed of the cash flow cycle by increasing the efficiency of employees who are in control of the process. The invoice creation process should be automated, if possible, in order to ensure maximum efficiency in the billing process. This will lead to faster turnaround times on pay received from those who owe you money.

APPENDIX 5: POSITIVE CASH FLOW AND GOOD DEBTOR CONTROL

Inventory improvement is another way that some businesses decrease the time between cash cycles. Inventory ties up a significant portion of your potential working capital until it is sold. Businesses that make use of inventory optimisation technologies and collaboration tools can cut down on their lag time between cash flow cycles. Inventory optimization technologies are designed to provide businesses with a tool that tells them what the perfect mixture of inventory and cash on hand happens to be. Too much of one or the other can adversely affect cash flow in either the long term or the short term.

As a small business owner, do you struggle to collect customer payments on time?

If so, you may want to include payment terms with your sales.

Payment terms are guidelines you set for customers. The terms tell your customers how, when, and what to pay you. If a customer does not pay you the total amount by the scheduled date, you can choose to charge interest.

Usually, you outline your payment terms in an invoice to avoid collection problems. You should let your customers know about the terms before you send invoices, such as late payment processing or account keeping fee and interest for late payment. Also, include terms in the invoices.

No matter your business's size, payment terms are a good idea for every sale. Payment terms prevent misunderstandings between you and your customers. They also offer an explanation for the amounts you charge.

Terms of payment help you get paid faster. They give customers a due date to pay you by. Without a deadline, customers might delay or forget to make payments.

One of our new customers had the experience of his larger customers using him as 'their bank' whilst he had to pay interest on his overdraft to keep his business going. By introducing new credit terms and informing his customers with a personally addressed letter and including those same new credit terms on their next invoice, he managed to reduce his debtor days from invoice to payment by 73%! He also requested a 50% deposit for larger orders enabling him to be cashflow positive and not even use his overdraft – how good is that?

Slow-paying customers can make it difficult to project and manage your cash flow. Cash flow is the amount of money coming in and out of your business. You may make steady sales, but your cash flow will weaken as customer payments lag. When your cash flow slows to a crawl, so does your business. A negative operating cash flow isn't sustainable, so how can you shape up your finances?

Payment term tips to improve cash flow

Are you using efficient payment terms to collect money?

No?

Well then, consider these tips for inclusion in your new payment terms and watch how quickly things will turn around and improve:

1. Use clear communication

    Before you begin work or deliver products to a customer, discuss your payment terms. Define your payment expectations, and what customers can trust you to do, to reduce communication issues.

APPENDIX 5: POSITIVE CASH FLOW AND GOOD DEBTOR CONTROL

Be clear and polite with your customers. Whether a payment is negotiated or standard, make sure the terms are agreed upon before moving forward.

2. Put payment terms in writing

It's essential to write down your payment terms. Doing this shows proof of your agreement with the customer. The customer also has a physical reminder of the payment information.

Make sure you get all the details of the sale when you write down your terms. This could include the customer's information, the scope of the work, and the purchase order number. Define when you expect to be paid and where customers should send payments.

3. Shorten the net days

Net days means the customer must pay the total invoice amount within a certain number of days after you send the invoice. Most industries have a standard amount of net days for payment terms (e.g., net 30).

Why? Who says you have to?

If you provide awesome customer service, exceptional delivery times and a quality product you will be in demand and can then set your own payment terms.

With new customers use cash on delivery, completion or at the end of the appointment. If you are a small business you don't have the luxury of time to do credit checks to see if they have a poor history of paying their bills!

Use a shorter time span for your business 7 days or 14 days and see the difference to your cash flow.

When you reduce the number of net days, you often receive the payment faster. The faster you receive payments, the stronger your cash flow is.

Keep in mind that not all customers will pay on time. With a net 30 days term, a late payment could stretch on for nearly two months before you're fully paid. If a customer is late with a short payment terms deadline (e.g., net 15 days term), you still might receive the payment within a month's time.

4. Set the number of days to pay

   When you set a deadline, use the number of days you expect to be paid by, not a distinct due date. For example, instead of saying you want to be paid by April fourth, say you want to be paid within 15 business days.

   When you name a specific pay date, it's easier to mark the day on the calendar and forget it. Instead of paying by the date, customers are more likely to pay on the date. While customers may pay on time, they are less likely to pay early. An on-time payment is great, but an early payment is better.

5. Use an early discount incentive (you shouldn't have to discount but this might be a last resort type option)

   Positive incentives, such as discounts, may motivate customers to pay faster. Giving the customer a percent off the total bill can speed up your cash flow.

   For example, you could offer 2% off the total for a payment received within 10 days of invoicing. Discounting a small percentage off can encourage customers without costing you a lot of revenue.

APPENDIX 5: POSITIVE CASH FLOW AND GOOD DEBTOR CONTROL

These five tips for improved payment terms could improve your cash flow. If you change your payment terms, notify your customers well before sending them invoices. Otherwise, you might find you have a real problem trying to enforce legal proceedings for recovery down the track if the debts prove to be difficult to collect!

Working capital days is an interesting number to monitor. Basically, working capital days measures the number of days between you paying for your cost of sales, and receiving payment from your customer.

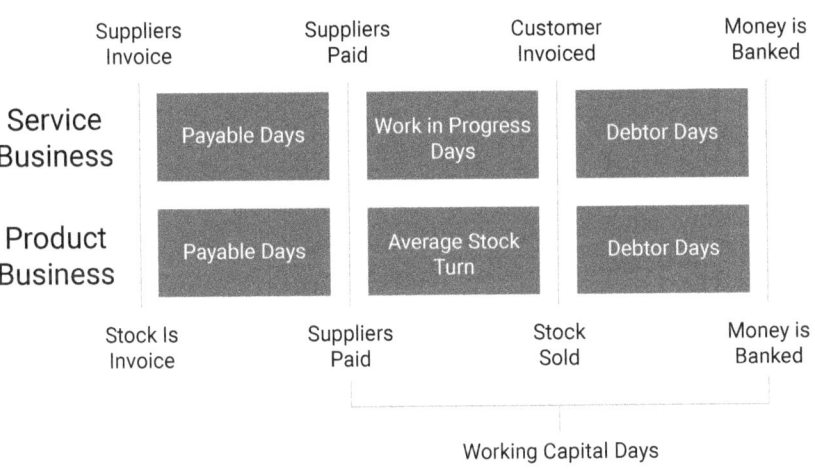

Consider focusing on these five areas to really improve your cash flow:

1. **The Goal is to Reduce Working Capital Days**

   The shorter the Working Capital Days are the better your cash flow will be as the cash is locked or "tied up" in working capital for the least amount of time.

   So if we increase Payable Days, and reduce both Work in Progress Days and Debtor Days, this will reduce working capital days and improve our business' cash flow.

   Your goal – aim to have negative working capital days, it is possible!

2. **Calculating Working Capital Days**

   As working capital is made up of other figures, we'll need to work out what the following numbers are:
   1. Payable Days
   2. Work in Progress Days or Average Stock Days
   3. Debtor Days

3. **Payable Days (or Creditors Days)**

$$\text{Payable Days} = \frac{\text{Payables at end of month}}{\text{Cost of Sales during month}} \times \text{no. days in month}$$

Although, technically, working capital days don't include payable days, the date that you pay your suppliers is the 'start day' of working capital days.

So what that means is, if we extend our payment terms with suppliers, we're shortening our working capital days if all else stays the same.

It's important to measure these days, because negotiating more favourable credit terms can reduce cash flow pressure and buy you some extra time!

4. **Work in Progress Days or Average Stock Days**

    Depending on your type of business, whether service (WIP Days) or selling products (Average Stock Days).

    For the service business, WIP days is "turnaround time" or the time from when the job comes in the door to when it is delivered to the customer.

$$\text{Average Stock Days} = \frac{\text{Days in month}}{} \div \frac{\text{Cost of Sales}}{\text{Average Stock \$}}$$

$$\text{where} \quad \text{Average Stock \$} = \frac{\text{Opening Stock} + \text{Closing Stock}}{2}$$

For businesses who carry stock, reducing the number of days your stock is sitting on your shelf (and tying up your cash until it is sold!) requires skill and experience

The formula above can be used for a service business if you put a dollar figure on your WIP.

Without a dollar figure of your WIP, you will need to measure your turnaround time using a visual scoreboard or workflow management system. Turnaround time is critical not only for cash flow, but is extremely important in keeping your customers happy.

5. **Debtor Days**

Debtor days is fairly similar in process to calculating payable days.

Debtor days is calculating using the following formula:

$$\text{Debtor Days} = \frac{\text{Receivables at end of month}}{\text{Sales during month}} \times \text{no. days in month}$$

Interestingly, outstanding debts can be a deterrent to purchasing from you again. That is, if they owe you money but still need goods or services in your field, some customers will choose to go to your competitor. This is simply because they're embarrassed that they haven't paid the bill, or that they can't afford to pay the bill despite needing more goods or services.

Can you remember renting videos from a video store? Well the old video store provides the perfect example of this. When people used to rent videos, many returned them late. As such, many stores charged late fees. Often, if a regular customer knows they have late fees due at one store, they will simply go to another and join up!

This issue can be avoided if you keep a tight control on your debtors, keep them at a minimum, and never let them accrue too much!

Even on briefly reviewing these ideas, you've probably found many ways to keep your customers coming back more often. Some you may have heard of or tried, others not.

Regardless, it's important to start implementing these ideas and you will start to see the benefits of doing so.

Appendix 6

Margin Tables

The following table indicates the increase in sales required to compensate for a price discounting policy. For example, if your gross margin is 30% and you reduce price by 10%, you need sales volume to increase by 50% to maintain your initial profit. Rarely has such a strategy worked in the past, and it's unlikely that it will work in the future.

APPENDIX 6: MARGIN TABLES

If your present margin is...

And reduce your price by...	20%	25%	30%	35%	40%	45%	50%	55%	60%
\ To produce the same profit, you must increase your sales volume by...									
2%	11%	9%	7%	6%	5%	5%	4%	4%	4%
4%	25%	19%	15%	13%	11%	10%	9%	8%	7%
6%	43%	43%	25%	21%	18%	15%	14%	12%	11%
8%	67%	47%	36%	30%	25%	22%	19%	17%	15%
10%	100%	67%	50%	40%	33%	29%	25%	22%	20%
12%	150%	92%	67%	52%	43%	36%	32%	28%	25%
14%	233%	127%	88%	67%	54%	45%	39%	34%	30%
16%	400%	178%	114%	84%	67%	55%	47%	41%	36%
18%	900%	257%	150%	106%	82%	67%	56%	49%	43%
20%	*	400%	200%	133%	100%	80%	67%	57%	50%
25%	*	*	500%	250%	167%	125%	100%	83%	71%
30%	*	*	*	600%	300%	200%	150%	120%	100%

The next table shows the amount by which your sales would have to decline following a price increase before your gross profit is reduced below its previous level. At a 30% margin and a 10% increase in price, you could sustain a 25% reduction in sales volume before your profit is reduced to the previous level... you would have to lose 1 out of every 4 customers!

If your present margin is...

	20%	25%	30%	35%	40%	45%	50%	55%	60%
To produce the same profit, you could reduce your sales volume by...

And increase your price by...

	20%	25%	30%	35%	40%	45%	50%	55%	60%
2%	9%	7%	6%	5%	5%	4%	4%	4%	3%
4%	17%	14%	12%	10%	9%	8%	7%	7%	7%
6%	23%	19%	17%	15%	13%	12%	11%	10%	9%
8%	29%	24%	21%	19%	17%	15%	14%	13%	12%
10%	33%	29%	25%	22%	20%	18%	17%	15%	14%
12%	38%	32%	29%	26%	23%	21%	19%	18%	17%
14%	41%	36%	32%	29%	26%	24%	22%	20%	19%
16%	44%	39%	35%	31%	29%	26%	24%	23%	21%
18%	47%	42%	38%	34%	31%	29%	26%	25%	23%
20%	50%	44%	40%	36%	33%	31%	29%	27%	25%
25%	56%	50%	45%	42%	38%	36%	33%	31%	29%
30%	60%	55%	50%	46%	43%	40%	38%	35%	33%

Appendix 7

Performance Standards for your Phone

To get a sense of exactly how important it is, let's imagine your business receives 20 phone calls a day. That's 100 to 200 a week, or over 5,000 a year!

And that's over 5,000 opportunities to create a marvellous and memorable impression.

From here on in, it really is important to think of every phone call your company receives as an opportunity – an opportunity to let the caller know they are indeed talking with one of the most terrific companies in your industry.

At the same time, the other vital point is to realise callers never talk with your 'company' as such. They talk with people – YOU and your team members. This means that you and every single team member are directly responsible for your corporate image.

And that image is most obvious and critical on the phone. Interestingly, that impression starts BEFORE you even pick up the phone. That's why these first few performance standards are so important.

Performance Standard #1: SMILE to the point of a GRIN before you pick up your phone.

This standard ensures that you or a team member can't answer the phone sounding grumpy, or with a tone of voice that suggests, 'I'd get lots of work done if you people would just stop calling me!' Or worse yet, sounding exasperated because they're busy. You really can hear a smile over the phone, and it makes the customers feel welcome, which instantly tells them they made the right choice by calling you over your competitors.

Performance Standard #2: Answer your phone on the second ring.

Most customers find it very annoying when a phone rings and rings and rings. Often, they'll think they've made a mistake and try again, only to have it ring and ring and then be answered by someone who wishes the phone hadn't interrupted them! This standard shows potential customers you really are eager to talk with them and that you're 'on the ball.'

Next, it's important to actually create a great first impression. Clearly, the actual words you use on the phone are a major part of that first impression. So Performance Standard #3 is to answer the phone in the following way:

APPENDIX 7: PERFORMANCE STANDARDS FOR YOUR PHONE

Performance Standard #3: "Good [morning/afternoon/evening], [optional location], this is [your first name and your last name]"

The 'good morning, afternoon, or evening' is important because it gets the phone call off to a good star, doesn't it? It is a positive, polite statement (one that is welcoming) that you virtually can't say without having to try to sound at least a little bit genuine!

Also, think about when you've made a phone call. It's often easy to miss the first few words somebody says, isn't it? That's why, we sometimes have to ask, "Is this ABC Company?" just to check we've reached the right number. 'Good morning' means a person doesn't miss anything important and gives them a chance to settle!

Next, the 'optional location' is important to let people know what business or department they've reached. It's optional only in terms of what you specifically say, for example:

"Good morning, Ceebeks Business Solutions for GOOD, this is Angela Tirabassi."
"Good afternoon, Accountants Department, this is Ima Counter.
"Good evening, Donald Trumpets's office, this is Hope Less."

'This is' is critical because it acts as a trigger. You see, when the caller hears 'this is,' they know you're not going to say something like, "Good morning, XYZ Company, this is Tuesday." Inherently, they know a name is about to be spoken. So much so, it triggers them to get ready to respond.

Then when they hear the next step, your full name, in almost 80% of cases, people will AUTOMATICALLY respond with their full name right back.

In fact, it will usually be the first thing they say, like this:

"Oh, it's Merissa Pye here, I'm calling to find out about..."

The use of your full name is pivotal to create an impression of someone who knows what they're doing. And that's important because, again, it builds confidence.

Think about this for a moment. People in more senior positions usually tend to use their full name, don't they? Whereas receptionists or secretaries tend to say something like "Georgia speaking."

A full name conveys a sense of authority. This is critically important because people tend to want to talk with someone they BELIEVE has the authority to help them.

You see, the caller is phoning only because they have a problem they want someone to solve. And the authority that's conveyed with the full name is critically important for building trust.

The important point here is to NOT add anything to the end of your name – no 'may I help you,' no 'speaking.'

There is only one exception to this rule, and this is for a true receptionist. Someone whose task is to always welcome the caller and transfer the call.

For a true receptionist the greeting can be modified to:

"Good [morning/afternoon/evening], [optional location], this is [your receptionist's first name] speaking."

Again, the reason this works here is simply this: Using a first name followed by the word speaking implies that the person is NOT in a position of authority. As such, they may not be able to help, except to put you through to the right person.

APPENDIX 7: PERFORMANCE STANDARDS FOR YOUR PHONE

This is the ONLY time the 'first name, speaking' greeting is used. Everywhere else in your enterprise, the full-name greeting really is essential to win your potential customers over.

So there are some simple tips that really do make a difference to your customers' first impression.

Let your team know you're not asking them to do this new style forever and a day – you'd like them do it this way for the next 21 days so they can judge for themselves what will happen. Let them know, too, that most people who've done it this way will NEVER go back to their 'old ways' – they just get so much out of it.

Point out, too, that if your team members were to join a new company where someone said to them, "By the way, this the way we all answer the phone here," they'd automatically conform to become part of the team! Given that, ask them to give it their best shot.

Some other ideas for you and your team

NEVER. Repeat NEVER use the following phrases:

He's in a meeting
She's out to lunch.
He's not in.
She's on vacation.
Can I take a message?

Why?
Because it really annoys people!
In fact, it drives some people crazy!

Think about the last time you tried to reach someone and got these sorts of responses. It *was* annoying, wasn't it? It just sounds like an excuse used to not talk with them doesn't it?

If I call to speak with someone because I need help or I have a problem that, in my mind, needs an urgent solution, I don't want to hear that someone is out and about enjoying themselves having lunch or, worse yet, on vacation with no foreseeable return!

Furthermore, if he or she is in a meeting, I want that meeting interrupted or, better yet, ended, because my problem or need is paramount – it's one of the most important things to me and as such needs addressing THIS INSTANT.

Or if she's not in (when I want her to be), I might think 'Well, where is she anyway when I need her help?'

When I hear these sorts of messages, I'll often want to give the receptionist or team member I'm talking with an earful about how difficult it is to get in touch with that person, how disorganised it seems, and so on.

The phrases below help you address customers in these situations in a way that lets them know they'll be assisted.

Don't say...	Say this instead...
He's in a meeting.	Clint's with someone right now.
She's out to lunch.	Angela's not actually in the office right now.

APPENDIX 7: PERFORMANCE STANDARDS FOR YOUR PHONE

He's not in.	Paul's not in the office right now.
She's on vacation.	Merissa's on vacation and will be back on (date).
Can I take a message?	In the meantime, maybe there's some way I can help?

The phrase *"in the meantime, maybe there's some way I can help?"* is absolutely indispensable!

It lets the caller know that you, as a business, are NOT just going to leave them in the lurch, that you really would like to help any way you can even if He or She is away or out of the office, for example. Or even if it just means you take a message and promise to "deliver it to them as soon as they get in," your customers will, more often than not, be appeased.

Acknowledgements

Paul Dunn – mentor, friend and chairman of B1G1 – Business for Good
Alan Weiss – consultant and author
Peter Drucker – The Practice of Management
Bernadette Jiwa – Meaningful
Michael Gerber – The E-Myth Revisited – Why Most Small Businesses Don't Work and What to Do About It
Seth Godin – The Purple Cow
Simon Sinek – Start with WHY
Adam Houlahan – The LinkedIn Playbook
Edward W Demming – American engineer
Daniel Priestly – Key Persons of Influence
Sir Richard Branson – Entrepreneur
Robert B Cialdini – Yes! 50 Scientifically Proven Ways to Be Persuasive
Gary Keller – The ONE Thing
Steven R Covey – The 7 Habits of Highly Successful People

About the Author

Just like most business owners he has a life outside of work. A spouse, three teenage daughters (yes, he agrees he is in trouble!), a veggie garden, chooks, cats, dogs and a tropical garden that he is trying to create in a temperate gardening climate zone!

He is a passionate Blues (AFL) supporter and Washington Wizards (NBA) supporter. He has represented Victoria at the Australian U20 Basketball Championships, run in the 10km New York Midnight Run held at New Years Eve through Central Park, trekked in the Himalayas and scuba dived Julian Rocks Marine Reserve at Byron Bay and Ewen Ponds Conservation Park in South Australia.

He loves singing and performing arts and has "tread the boards" for over a decade with the Warrnambool Theatre Company.

And in his spare time he has also been a qualified fitness and aerobic instructor!

He is a self-described 'lifestyle' accountant, passionate about making an impact on one person's lifestyle at a time!

He holds a Bachelor of Business from Latrobe University and a Graduate Diploma in Management Accounting with Deakin University.

He has over 35 years' experience as a practising CPA, holds an authorised representative accreditation with MyPlanner Pty Ltd, a credit representative accreditation with Outsource Financial Pty Ltd a certified Xero advisor, an accredited certified Inbound user of Hubspot and is a graduate of the Results Accounting Systems boot camp!

He was a charter member and president of the Rotary Club of Warrnambool Daybreak and served Rotary International for over 10 years.

He is the team leader at Ceebeks Business Solutions for GOOD, an accounting and business development specialist business based in Southwest Victoria in Australia that he started in 1990.

He is also a foundation member of the National Tax & Accountants Association (NTAA) also a foundation member of global movement Accountants 4 Good.

Ceebeks Business Solutions for GOOD is a multi-award winning business and was featured in Steve Pipe's 2015 UK publication 'The World's Most Inspiring Accountants' and in his new upcoming UK publication 'The World's Best Accountancy Practices' and also in Adam Houlahan's 2016 publication 'The LinkedIn Play Book.

They are corporate volunteers at Warrnambool and District Food Share where a team member spends 2 hours every Wednesday morning assisting with repurposing donated food into hampers for those less fortunate in the Southwest Victorian community, regular blood donors, 28 year supporters of World Vision and lifetime members of global giving initiative B1G1 – Business for Good.

Special Offer

For a business owner like you, life's 'little' challenges can be far more than that.

Being in business can be tough. That's why the 'little' challenges most people face don't compare to those you deal with day to day! There's often the long hours and the 'fire fighting' to contend with all of which can make or break your business. And that's just to start.

If you're like most you spend a lot of your time working **IN** your business. Dealing with customers, team members, suppliers, creditors, bankers, taxes, paperwork, sales, managing your costs, advertising, marketing and the list just goes on and on all because you had one great idea.

An idea of what your business could be – how it could improve your life and build your financial independence but after all that when do you find time to make that idea a reality?

Well, as a valued reader of this book, we have secured you a special invitation to join The 'Chasers Getting Results™' program.

The 'Chasers Getting Results™' program (CGR for short) produced by Chris Beks from Ceebeks Business Solutions for GOOD gives you the opportunity to 'put out some of those fires'.

You will be able to connect with other program attendees to discuss ideas, collaborate and share what's working for you with our Facebook Community Group.

And quickly (for just an hour or two a month) discover new ways to grow your business and make it that much more valuable. Together with the team from Ceebeks Business Solutions for GOOD and other members of the 'CGR' program you'll finally have the chance to truly achieve your goals while you manage your business day to day more easily.

Realise your vision by joining 'Chasers Getting Results™'

To finally bring that idea or 'vision' to life it's crucial you work **ON** improving your business – like creating systems and strategies to solve many of the challenges you face AND make the most of often hidden opportunities.

By focussing on proven business building strategies and new ideas, CGR helps you discover the opportunities right at your doorstep and tackles the challenges holding you back. This helps you build an even better business so your business grows, your profits improve, and your life and lifestyle get better.

Invaluable new ideas, information and support for you

CGR has been specifically created to give you a new level of support and new strategies for growth. Like how to plan for the future, reach your goals, improve your marketing, sales, management, team work, productivity, systems and financial position. All designed to make your business more profitable and more valuable, in an easy to implement and affordable program available right here in your virtual community.

To qualify to join 'Chasers Getting Results™' you must:

1. Want to improve your business significantly over the next 72 months.
2. Commit to spending a minimum of just 2 hours a month working **ON** your business.
3. Be interested in finding new ways to solve challenges.
4. Be willing to explore the hidden opportunities that DO exist in your business right now.

Experience this new kind of support – free.

So you can discover 'Chasers Getting Results™' for yourself email us at Ceebeks Business Solutions for GOOD now at cgr@ceebeks.com to find out more and get access to your first FREE module as an Introduction to the course.

Ceebeks
Business Solutions for GOOD

25 Banyan Street, Warrnambool 3280
P: 035561 2643
E: cgr@ceebeks.com
W: **www.ceebeks.com**

www.ingramcontent.com/pod-product-compliance
Lightning Source LLC
Chambersburg PA
CBHW050310010526
44107CB00055B/2185